As a devoutly committed foodie, I read Rachel Patterson's *A Kitchen Witch's World of Magical Food* over afternoon tea in front of a log fire – and heartedly endorse her view that 'food is magical, not just because of the amazing tastes, flavours and aromas but also for the magical properties it holds'. She also reveals how Craft can be tempered with reverence, mirth and merriment, not to mention gastronomic enjoyment – while her recipes take us a long way from the traditional 'cakes and ale' of the post-ritual feast. I also liked the fact that she caters for us meat-eaters in the text without any hint of censure. An excellent addition to her 'Kitchen Witch' series and a book that would make the perfect gift for pagan (and not so pagan) friends to read with relish.
Melusine Draco, Moon Books author and Principal of Coven of the Scales

Rachel Patterson has provided a clear and concise book that shows the kitchen as a sacred space, and cooking as a truly magical art. *A Kitchen Witch's World of Magical Food* is easy to use as inspiration, reference, or as an introduction to casting with your cast iron pans. I will be working my way through the recipes!
Romany Rivers, author of *The Woven Word*

A Kitchen Witch's World of Magical Food is an enchanting look at the magic and mystery of food, from the power of tea to edible flowers, from seasonal treats to food poppets. A delightful book full of recipes and food lore that would be a great addition to any magical practitioner's library.
Morgan Daimler, author of *Fairy Witchcraft* and *Pagan Portals: The Morrigan*

A Kitchen Witch's World of Magical Food

A Kitchen Witch's World of Magical Food

Rachel Patterson

Winchester, UK
Washington, USA

First published by Moon Books, 2015
Moon Books is an imprint of John Hunt Publishing Ltd., Laurel House, Station Approach,
Alresford, Hants, SO24 9JH, UK
office1@jhpbooks.net
www.johnhuntpublishing.com
www.moon-books.net

For distributor details and how to order please visit the 'Ordering' section on our website.

Text copyright: Rachel Patterson 2014

ISBN: 978 1 78279 854 5
Library of Congress Control Number: 2015931660

A CIP catalogue record for this book is available from the British Library.

Design: Lee Nash

Printed and bound by CPI Group (UK) Ltd, Croydon, CR0 4YY, UK

We operate a distinctive and ethical publishing philosophy in all
areas of our business, from our global network of authors to
production and worldwide distribution.

CONTENTS

The Magic of Food

Food is magical, not just because of the amazing tastes, flavours and aromas, but also for the magical properties it holds. The magic starts with the choice of food to use and it can then be added in while you are preparing and cooking, then the magic unfolds as people enjoy your food. Dishes can be created for specific intents, moon phases, and rituals; to celebrate sabbats or just to bring the magic into your family meal. Many food ingredients can also be used very successfully in magical workings in the form of offerings, medicine pouches, witches' bottles and poppets.

When you are cooking, whether it is baking, stirring, kneading or whatever process it involves, make sure to add the magic as you go. Stir deosil (clockwise) to bring in positive energy and widdershins (anti-clockwise) to banish. Think about your intent, desires and wishes as you make the dish; add your energy to it, visualise the outcome as you add the ingredients and you can even chant a blessing or a spell as you make it.

Think about how you work in the kitchen and see if you can add a magical spin to it, there are some ideas in my book *Pagan Portals: Kitchen Witchcraft*, so I don't want to duplicate the information, but to give you some ideas to get started with:

- Chopping – this releases frustration and emotions... just be careful.
- Peeling fruit and vegetables – as you take off the skin release old habits and negative energy revealing the fresh, clean surface underneath and a refreshed, revitalised you.
- When you mix or shake any recipe... dance and sing.
- Slow stirring of sauces brings peace and calm.
- Mixing and whisking brings things together; use your visualisation skills.

This book includes the more commonly used foods, herbs and spices and it also contains magical information for meat. Whether you are vegetarian, vegan or a meat eater, animal welfare should be paramount. For those of us who choose to eat meat I wholeheartedly believe that we should honour the animal that gave its life. If your joint of meat or bird has the bones make full use of them after you have eaten. Boil the bones to make stock and then dry them to use in magical workings.

If you are able to purchase your meat direct from the farm you may even be able to get hold of the skin as well to create something useful with. If you get the feathers from a bird make sure you use them as well. All life is precious and if one has been taken to be used as food then we owe it to the creature to use everything it has provided for us.

If you can afford to, I would encourage you to purchase organic or free range meat; the animal deserves the best life that it can have. If you don't have a farm shop local to you seek out your local butcher where you should be able to purchase meat that has a history. The butcher will know exactly where the meat came from and how the animal was treated. They are also really helpful in advising and suggesting cuts of meat to use and how to cook them.

Your Magical Kitchen Space
Some people love the kitchen, some hate it. I guess it depends whether you like to cook or not, but even if you just use the microwave to heat up a ready meal (gasp!) the kitchen is quite often the centre of a home. I do believe that part of cooking successfully is feeling comfortable in the space that you work in. Although I often dream of a huge farmhouse kitchen with space for a large table that everyone can gather around… my kitchen is not that. It is a small space in a terraced house, but – and here is the important part – it is MY space. Everything I need is to hand and I know where everything is; I am very comfortable there, in

some ways it is even my haven. So no matter what the size, age or state of your kitchen – make it yours. It doesn't have to be fancy or expensive, but do what you can to make it feel like your own.

I know I have said this before, but I do find that 'making like Snow White' really does help. You don't have to be a total clean freak, but keeping your kitchen clean and tidy helps the magic flow. If the kitchen is in total chaos then that is the kind of magic that you will produce. If the kitchen is dirty and unclean then the magic gets stuck in all the debris. I also find that keeping everything tidy and organised helps when you are actually cooking, with everything to hand and knowing where it all is helps with the flow. And, let's face it, if you walk into your kitchen ready to do some work and it looks like an explosion in a cake factory you won't really feel inspired to create something beautiful.

I've also said this before and it might sound completely loony, but make friends with your appliances. You don't have to buy them birthday cards or anything (that would be mad…) but add your positive energy to them to keep them working properly and helping you in the kitchen.

Food is a source of energy, but it can also be full of magic. Try – and I say try because we can't always be sweetness and light 100% of the time – but try to cook when you are feeling happy and content. Cooking when you are cross or angry not only transfers the negative energy to the food and therefore into the people who eat it, but it also doesn't help the cooking process. If you are upset and grumpy when you cook the chances of your dish turning out a disaster are much higher. If you are feeling less than your best, take a few moments first, clear your mind, ground yourself and just breathe…

Bless Those Pots and Pans

When you purchase or are given a new pot, pan or utensil it is a nice idea to give them a quick cleanse, after all you don't know who has picked them up in the store to look at them or what snotty child has wiped his fingers over them in passing... ewwww! Give them a good wash in soapy water, and then I like to sprinkle mine with salt water then dry them. You can also smudge them if you like. If you feel poetic you could also say a little blessing or chant for them: 'To my little baking pot, help me cook perfectly a lot.' OK, you must be able to come up with something far more lyrical than that, but you get the idea.

Kitchen Altar

I have a small altar on the wall in my kitchen; it is actually a green man shelf. It isn't very big and just has a tiny vase on that I put a fresh flower in (it is only big enough for one flower) and has tiny representations of the elements – a pebble, a shell, a small red crystal and a tiny feather. When I start any cooking, whether is it a family meal or a witchy lotion or potion, I give the altar a nod and ask for blessings. It does not have to be a huge or ornate altar flowing with velvet and gold tassels – just the corner of a shelf would do, even just a vase with a flower in. Something that just represents deity, the divine or the universal energy that can aid you in your cookery endeavours.

Kitchen Rituals

We all have rituals that we perform throughout the day, even simple ones such as brushing our teeth before getting into the shower. Rituals are actions that we perform with a purpose or intent in mind. A kitchen ritual need not be complicated and sometimes the simple ones work the best. Your kitchen ritual may just be like mine... I give a nod to the altar in my kitchen and ask the goddess to bless my cooking – it really is that simple. It might be that you like to light a candle before you start your culinary escapades or you might like to pour yourself a glass of wine, these are all rituals.

You could visualise as you wash your hands – allow the water to rinse away all the worries and stresses of the day.

Smudge your kitchen before you begin cooking; just a quick waft around with an incense stick would do the trick.

Light a candle and hold it up to each direction and ask for the blessings from the four elements.

Come up with a short chant to ask deity to bless your cooking skills and the food that you create.

Think about what works for you.

Kitchen Deities

There are many deities associated with the home, hearth and cooking. If you wanted to work with one to help you with your culinary skills or just to give you support and add their energies to your magical food, you could look at the following list. A lot of them are associated with fire as that has a big connection to the kitchen or to the harvest and food:

Agnaya – Hindu goddess of fire

Agni – Indian fire god of home and hearth

Ayabba – African goddess of the hearth

Brighid – Irish goddess of the hearth and fire

Ceres – Roman corn goddess

Cerridwen – Celtic goddess associated with the cauldron

Chantico – Aztec goddess of hearth fires

Dugnai – Slavic goddess of the home and bread

Ephesus – Greek god of fire

Erce – English goddess of blessings

Fornax – Roman goddess of the oven

Freya – Norse goddess of fire and domestic arts

Frigg – Norse goddess associated with domestic arts

Fuchi – Japanese goddess of fire

Hestia – Greek goddess of fire and the hearth and home

Hehsui-no-kami – Japanese kitchen goddess

Hyang Api – Indonesian god of fire

Hyang Kehen – Indonesian god of the hearth
Li – Chinese goddess of fire
Mama Occlo – Inca goddess of domestic arts
Ogetsu-im-no-kami – Japanese goddess of food
Okitsu-hime – Japanese kitchen goddess
Ong Tao – Asian god of hearth and home
Pele – Hawaiian goddess of fire
Pirua – Peruvian goddess of corn
Pomona – Roman goddess of orchards and gardens
Saule – Slavic goddess of the hearth and domestic arts
Tsao Wang – Chinese god of hearth and home
Ut – Siberian goddess of the hearth
Vesta – Roman goddess of domestic fires and the hearth

The Magic of Tea

We all know that blissful moment of putting our feet up at the end of a hard day and sipping a hot cup of soothing tea. Relaxing, calming and apparently the answer to every situation: 'Have a cup of tea, it will make you feel better.' But tea can also be extremely magical, especially if you create the blends yourself and tie them in with your magical intent.

I have a beautiful teapot that has a built in infuser, but you can get small metal infusers for individual cups of tea and these are brilliant for popping your tea blends into or just use a normal teapot and a strainer. You will want to use one of these methods otherwise you will be spitting bits of herb and spice out…

I think there is something very magical about the whole process of making tea, especially if you make a bit of an effort rather than just throwing a teabag into a cup and filling it up. It can become a small ritual in itself.

The Japanese have a tea ceremony called Chanoyu, Sado or Ocha. The whole event from preparation to serving and drinking the tea (a green tea called Matcha) is part of the ritual. It isn't all about drinking the tea, it is about the care and attention that goes into it, the serving of it and the appreciation.

The Japanese tea ceremony is for creating relaxation, communication (if you are serving guests), connections with your surroundings and the elements, to create harmony, but ultimately the aim is to make that deep spiritual connection that you get from drinking the tea in silent contemplation. Almost as if the process from preparation, serving and drinking is all part of a ritual to send you into a meditative spiritual state. The Japanese tea ceremony philosophy is one of harmony, respect, purity and tranquillity.

I like to take the idea of the Japanese tea ceremony and make it a very magical one. This is easily done and can involve the whole ritual process of casting a circle, calling the quarters and even requesting the presence of deity if you so wish, but it can also just be kept very simple and run along the lines of casting a spell or simply spending time in meditation.

Create your space, the ambience and the setting – this could just be sitting in your garden or at your kitchen table, but maybe put a vase of fresh flowers on the table and a nice tablecloth. You could put on some nice plinky plonky meditation music if you are indoors.

Select your tea blend. There are a huge amount of fantastic herbal tea blends in the shops, but herbal teas are also super easy to make for yourself using herbs and spices you have in your kitchen or garden.

Here are some simple ideas to get your creative side working:

Ginger – Truly simple… Just use a few slices of root ginger. Ginger has the magical properties of love, success and power.
Ginger and lemon – Use a few slices of root ginger and a slice of lemon (or a squeeze of lemon juice). Add in the magical properties of lemon and you get a double whammy of love and also friendship, purification and the power of the moon.
Cinnamon – Either cinnamon stick crushed or a sprinkle of ground cinnamon. This is a brilliant magical spice and brings in success, healing, psychic powers, protection, love and a spiritual connection.
Cardamom – Squish a couple of cardamom pods so that the hot water can get to the flavour of the black seeds inside and you will have yourself a hot drink that not only brings love, but also a powerful boost of lust too.
Clove – Two or three cloves per cup and you have yourself a protection, love and money tea blend, although it can be a bit 'medicinal' tasting on its own. I like to mix it with cardamom and fennel.
Fennel seed – Half a teaspoon of fennel seeds per cup brings

you a healing, purifying and protective cuppa.

Lemon balm – This makes a lovely lemon flavour tea (unsurprisingly). It grows like a mad thing in my garden so I just pick a handful of the leaves and pop them in a teapot. Lemon balm is brilliant for success, love and healing.

Mint – Could not be an easier tea to make, a few mint leaves and *et voilà* a cup of protective, healing, prosperity filled tea is yours for the sipping.

Rose petals – These can be used in tea blends as well (make sure to wash them first as you don't want green fly in your cup). Rose brings with it the magical power of love, psychic powers, luck, protection and healing.

Rosemary – This works well in tea blends, but be careful not to use too much otherwise it tastes like antiseptic... but it does have the magical properties of healing, purification, love, protection and that lust thing.

Sage – Very good for protection and wisdom and it also makes a good 'make a wish' cup of tea, but as with rosemary don't use too much as the flavour can be quite overpowering.

Thyme – One of my favourite flavours, thyme comes with healing, purifying powers that boost your psychic abilities and also bring love and courage.

Your usual cup of black tea has magical properties itself and is good for bringing courage and strength, but you can also use it as the base for tea blends if you don't fancy the herbal ones on their own.

If the taste of herbal tea on its own makes your face twist up in disgust you can try adding a teaspoonful of honey to sweeten the blend. And if you really can't stand the taste of a blend don't waste it... use it as magical floor wash.

Experiment with your ingredients, go with your own instincts, have fun and be creative with it.

Take some time to think about the blend you want and the

magical intent you need, then as you pour the boiling water onto the herbs and spices visualise your goal, desire or wish being activated by the water.

Allow the herbs to steep for about five minutes. Take this time to clear your thoughts and to ground and centre yourself.

When you are ready pour the tea into a nice cup, I prefer a china cup for tea – but that's just me, you might prefer a big builder's tea mug.

Hold the cup up and take a whiff of the scent as the steam rises from the cup, take deep breathes in and then sip… ahhhh… allow the hot tea to connect with your inner being. Allow it to flow and bring the energy it has to your body, mind and total being.

Enjoy a few moments of utter peace and calming bliss. Allow the world to carry on around you, leaving you to your own personal space and inner thoughts.

Once you have finished your tea return the used spices, tea leaves and herbs back to Mother Earth either via your garden or your compost heap.

And, of course, if you have a nice slice of cake to go with your cuppa… so much the better…

Tea Leaf Reading

Tea leaf reading, or tasseography, is fairly simple to do. First of all you need to make a cup of tea… that was pretty obvious wasn't it? You will need to use loose leaf tea made in a pot, let it steep for a few minutes (if you don't have loose leaf tea you can open up a tea bag). While the tea is brewing use this time to ground and centre yourself and allow your mind to become calm. Then pour yourself a cup of tea, a plain light colour cup is best.

Slowly sip the tea (avoiding the tea leaves). If you have a question in mind then think about it as you drink your tea.

Leave a small amount of tea in your cup, then hold your nearly empty cup in your hand and swirl it around three times.

The tea leaves should disperse around the inside of the cup. Carefully dump out the remaining liquid by turning your cup over into a saucer... wait for a count of three then turn your cup back over.

If your cup has a handle, begin reading the tea leaves from that point working clockwise, if it has no handle start at the 12 o'clock position.

Read what you see...

This can also be done with coffee grounds.

Seasonal Recipes

We seem to have lost the idea about eating seasonally with food being shipped all over the world and supermarkets stocking things such as strawberries in December. The thing is I don't believe the fruit and vegetables taste as nice out of season. Those December strawberries certainly look like strawberries, but they don't seem to have any taste. Of course the other benefit of eating fruits and vegetables in season is that the cost is lower. I would encourage you (if you don't already) to seek out your local farm shop or famers' market where you will be able to purchase organic seasonal fruit and vegetables.

The list below gives some idea of what is in season for each month, it is not totally comprehensive and obviously it will vary depending on where in the world you are but it gives a good basis to start:

Beltane – 30th April/1st May

Beltane is all about love, fertility and magic although not necessarily in that order and you don't have to be naked... not if you don't want to. Maidens dancing around the maypole and wearing flowers in their hair whilst handsome young suitors watch on... it is a celebration of life.

Food to celebrate this sabbat usually comes from the dairy (milk, butter, cheese etc), especially sweet kinds like custard and ice cream along with honey, oats, fresh fruit, salads, pork, spring vegetables and herbs (such as coriander, marjoram and tansy), chicken and fruit punch. I like to add chocolate into this one too, well I like to add it into most festivals, but it does contain dairy!

In the hedgerows during May you might find Alexanders, broom buds, chickweed, dandelions, fat hen, nettles, sorrel, wild rocket, horseradish, meadowsweet, wild fennel, wild garlic, elderflowers, primroses and, if you are lucky, some mushrooms.

Veggies that are in season around April/May time are globe artichokes, asparagus, broad beans, broccoli, cabbage, carrots, cauliflower, chard, greens, leeks, lettuce, onions, peas, potatoes, radish, spinach and watercress with the fruits in season being apricots and rhubarb.

Beltane Punch

Ingredients:
800ml (4 cups) of white wine
A big handful (1 cup) of woodruff (*Galium odoratum*) – freshly picked, washed and chopped (if you can get the buds and flowers as well all the better)
2 teaspoons of grated orange or lemon zest
2 teaspoons of sugar

Method:
Put the woodruff in a container and pour the wine over it, seal and keep in the fridge overnight. Then strain and keep the liquid, but discard the woodruff. Add the citrus zest and the sugar. Drink chilled, over ice works very well.

Magic of the ingredients:
Woodruff – Protection and prosperity
Orange – Luck, love and money
Lemon – Love, friendship and purification
Sugar – Sweetness of life
Wine – Fertility and money

Cheese and Herb Muffins
(Makes 12)

Ingredients:
270g/9 ½ oz plain flour

1 teaspoon salt

225/8 oz margarine or softened butter

75g 2 ½ oz grated cheese (a strong cheddar is good)

2 eggs

200ml/7 fl oz milk

3 teaspoons baking powder

Paprika

1 teaspoon dried herbs (or 2 teaspoons fresh chopped) – use what you have; thyme, marjoram or parsley all work well

Couple of tablespoons of extra cheese (grated)

12 paper muffin cases

Method:

Pre-heat the oven to 200C (Gas mark 6).

Rub the margarine into the flour and baking powder, and then add the cheese (I do this in a food mixer).

Beat the eggs into the milk and then add to the flour mixture and stir well. (The mixture will be sloppy and lumpy, don't worry it is supposed to be like that).

Place the paper muffin cases in a muffin tin and divide the mixture equally between them. (They will be quite full).

Sprinkle the extra grated cheese on the top of each one and add a pinch of paprika.

Bake in the oven for 20 minutes.

Magic of the ingredients:

Salt – Protection and warding negative energies

Paprika – Love and spicy passion!

Cheese and milk – Fertility and new beginnings

Parsley – Protection and purification

Thyme – Healing, love, purification, courage and psychic powers

Marjoram – Protection, love, happiness, health and money

The Summer Solstice/Litha – 20th-23rd June

Following on from the Beltane theme of celebrating life this sabbat is also about the abundance of beauty on our planet and all that she provides for us. Ideal food to share is honey, fresh vegetables, citrus fruit, summer fruits, summer squash, salads, herbs (such as basil, fennel, lavender, lemon verbena and thyme), ale and mead and of course if the weather is good... anything you can chuck on the BBQ.

This is the longest day and the shortest night of the year. This is a time to celebrate the completion of the cycle that began at the winter solstice – the sun is at the height of its power and although hopefully the hot days of summer are yet to come this is the point when the year starts to wane.

Connect to this moment by taking time to stop, be still and look back over the past few months, celebrate your achievements and acknowledge your failures, make sense of your actions and learn from them. Focus now on what you want to nurture and develop during the coming months.

While you are out and about enjoying the sunshine you may find broom buds, chickweed, fat hen, marsh samphire, nettles, sorrel, watercress, wild rocket, horseradish, chives, wild fennel, elderflowers and wild mushrooms in the fields and hedgerows.

Veggies that are in season during June/July are globe artichokes, asparagus, aubergine, beetroot, broad beans, broccoli, cabbages, carrots, cauliflower, courgettes, cucumber, fennel, French beans, garlic, lettuce, onions, peas, potatoes, radish, runner beans, spinach, tomatoes, turnips and watercress.

Fruits that are in season during June/July are apricots, blackcurrants, blackberries, blueberries, cherries, gooseberries, greengages, loganberries, melons, peaches, nectarines, raspberries, redcurrants, rhubarb, strawberries and whitecurrants.

Oaty Biscuits
(Makes 25)

Ingredients:
275g/9 ½ oz porridge oats
100g/3 ½ oz plain flour plus some extra for dusting
100g/3 ½ oz granulated sugar
50g/1 ¾ oz Demerara sugar
½ teaspoon bicarbonate of soda
A pinch of salt
225/8 oz margarine or softened butter
Flavours – you can add any of these (or come up with your own):
Lavender buds (1 tablespoon) but make sure it is from your own garden or for culinary use
Grated lemon zest (1 dessert spoon)
Fennel seeds (1 teaspoon) or lemon balm, finely chopped (1 tablespoon)
Vanilla – add a teaspoon of vanilla extract
I have even added a handful of chocolate chips, which works well too

Method:
Preheat the oven to 180C (Gas mark 4).

I use the porridge oats as they are, but if you prefer a smoother texture to your biscuits you can give them a whizz in the food processor first. Add all the other ingredients and mix until it comes together as dough (you may need to add a bit more flour at the end if the mixture is too sticky).

If you are adding any flavours add them at this stage too.

Lightly flour a work surface and roll the dough out to about 5mm thickness.

Cut them out using a cookie cutter and place them on a baking try (no need to grease or line the tray).

Bake the biscuits in the oven for 15-20 minutes, they should be pale golden in colour and slightly firm.

Cool them on a wire rack.

Magic of the ingredients:
Oats – Prosperity
Sugar – To make life sweet, love and lust
Salt – Protection and warding negative energies
Lavender – Love, protection, purification, happiness and peace
Lemon – Love, friendship and purification
Vanilla – Love and lust
Lemon balm – Success, love and healing
Fennel – Protection, purification and healing

Lemon and Mint Tea

Ingredients:
Handful of lemon balm (*Melissa officinalis*) leaves (washed)
Sprig of mint leaves
Teaspoon of honey
½ pint boiling water

Method:
Pour hot water onto the leaves and allow them to steep for five minutes, then strain and add a teaspoon of honey. This can be drunk hot or you can chill it in the fridge and add ice cubes for a refreshing cool drink.

Magic of the ingredients:
Lemon balm – Success, love and healing
Peppermint – Love, healing, purification, psychic powers

Lammas/Lughnasadh – 1st August
This is the time when our ancestors would have celebrated the first harvest and when the plants start sending out their seeds to

reproduce. When I think about this time of the year in my head it is filled with fields of grain ready for harvest, birds singing, the sun shining and all feels right with the world, but as I live in the UK the weather isn't always that reliable! The earth starts to prepares itself for the coming autumn, but don't dismay as it is a time to celebrate the abundance of the fruits and grains of the harvest and, indeed, of life itself.

Breads of all kinds feature strongly in the food theme for this sabbat along with any kind of grains washed down with a nice homemade wine or cider, then round off the meal with local fresh fruits and berries.

If you fancy a bit of foraging in the hedgerows you might find chickweed, fat hen, nettles, sorrel, wild rocket, horseradish, wild fennel, mushrooms and hazelnuts, but please make sure you have identified them correctly before ingesting any.

Veggies that are in season during August: globe artichokes, aubergines, beetroot, broad beans, broccoli, cabbage, carrots, cauliflower, courgettes, cucumber, fennel, French beans, garlic, leeks, lettuce, onions, peas, peppers, chillies, potatoes, pumpkin, squash, radish, runner beans, spinach, sweet corn, tomatoes, turnips and watercress.

Fruits that are in season during August: apples, apricots, black-currants, blackberries, blueberries, cherries, gooseberries, logan-berries, melons, peaches, nectarines, pears, plums, raspberries, redcurrants, rhubarb, strawberries and whitecurrants.

Herby Soda Bread

Ingredients:
500g/17 ½ oz plain flour (or you can use half plain, half wholemeal)
100g/3 ½ oz porridge oats
1 teaspoon bicarbonate of soda
1 teaspoon salt

1 teaspoon dried thyme or a good few sprigs of fresh thyme
(chopped)
25g/½ oz butter (or margarine)
500ml (1 pint) buttermilk

Method:
Preheat the oven to 200C/Gas 6/Fan 180C and sprinkle a dusting of flour over a baking sheet.

Mix all the dry ingredients together then rub in the butter. Pour in the buttermilk and mix with a knife then bring the dough together with your hands, treat it gently (it is a sticky dough). Shape it into a flat round loaf shape on the baking tray (about 8in in diameter).

Score a deep cross in the top of the loaf with a sharp knife – this is said to let the faeries or the bad spirits out. Bake in the centre of the oven for about 30 minutes until the bottom of the loaf sounds hollow when you tap it. Serve it warm with butter or cold with cheese and pickles.

Magic of the ingredients:
Salt – Protection and warding negative energies
Oats – Prosperity and money
Buttermilk – Fertility and new beginnings
Thyme – Healing, love, purification, courage and psychic powers

Lucky Heather Tea

Ingredients:
1 tablespoon dried heather flowers
250ml (½ pint) boiling water

Method:
Pop the heather flowers into a teapot, pour on boiling water and

leave to steep for about 5 minutes, strain and drink. You can add a little bit of honey if you wish.

Magic of the ingredients:
Heather – Luck and protection

The Autumn Equinox/Mabon – 20th-23rd September

The autumn equinox brings about the balance of equal day and night. It is a time to not only celebrate the second harvest of the year, but also to give thanks for all that we have, to look back on the warm summer months and all that they have brought us and to welcome the colder, darker days and nights ahead.

Bread features again for this celebration along with cake (of course, there always has to be cake), fruits, nuts and vegetables.

In the hedgerows during September you may find chickweed, fat hen, marsh samphire, nettles, sorrel, chives, horseradish, wild fennel, crab apples, elderberries, juniper berries, sloes, mushrooms, hazelnuts and walnuts.

Veggies in season during September: globe artichokes, aubergine, beetroot, borlotti beans, broad beans, broccoli, cabbage, carrots, cauliflower, celery, courgettes, cucumber, endive, fennel, French beans, garlic, leeks, lettuce, onions, parsnips, peas, peppers, chillies, potatoes, pumpkins, squash, radish, runner beans, spinach, swede, sweetcorn, tomatoes, turnips and watercress.

Fruit that is in season during September: apples, blackcurrants, blackberries, blueberries, cherries, damsons, greengages, loganberries, pears, plums, raspberries, redcurrants, rhubarb, strawberries, melons, peaches and nectarines.

Lemon Drizzle Cake (Gluten Free)

Ingredients:
200g/7 oz butter (or margarine)
200g/7 oz sugar

157g/5 ½ oz ground almonds
250g/9 oz mashed potato (cold)
Zest of 3 lemons
2 teaspoons baking powder (you can buy gluten free versions)

For the drizzle:
4 tablespoons sugar
Juice of one large lemon (or two small)

Method:
Preheat the oven to 180C/Gas mark 4/Fan 160C. Butter and line a deep 20cm round cake tin.

Beat the sugar and butter together until light and fluffy then gradually add the eggs, beating after each one. Fold in the ground almonds, cold mashed potato, lemon zest and baking powder.

Pour the mixture into the tin then bake for around 45 minutes. Cool for ten minutes then turn the cake out onto a wire rack. Mix the granulated sugar with the lemon juice and spoon over the top of the cake. Allow the cake to cool before serving.

Magic of the ingredients:
Sugar – To make life sweet, love and lust
Lemon – Love, friendship and purification
Almonds – Prosperity, money and wisdom
Potato – Healing and grounding

Enticing Elderberry Juice

Ingredients:
500m/1 pint fresh elderberries
2 tablespoons honey
1 tablespoon lemon juice
Spring of mint

Method:

Wash the elderberries and remove them from the stalks. Place the berries in a large jug or bowl and add the honey, lemon juice and the mint leaves. Add two pints of boiling water, give it a stir and then allow to cool. Strain the liquid into a clean jug giving the berries a bit of a squeeze with a spoon as you do so to get all the juice out. Serve the elderberry juice chilled over ice cubes.

Magic of the ingredients:

Elderberries – Prosperity, protection, healing

Honey – To make life sweet

Lemon – Love, friendship and purification

Mint – Money, healing, protection

Ketchup from the Hedge

Ingredients:

500g/17 ½ oz elderberries

500g/17 ½ oz blackberries, hawthorn haws, crab apples (mixture of all)

2 onions, chopped

2 teaspoons salt

300ml/10 ½ fl oz red wine vinegar

250g/9 oz light muscovado sugar

3 dried chillies

1 teaspoon peppercorns

1 teaspoon mustard seeds

3 slices root ginger

1 cinnamon stick, broken up

1 teaspoon lemon zest

Method:

Wash your fruit and pick out any stalks or leaves. Pop the fruit into a large pan with the onions, salt and vinegar.

Put the chillies, spices and lemon zest into a muslin bag, secure the top well and drop into the pan with the fruit.

Bring the pan slowly to the boil then reduce the heat and simmer gently (cover the top partly with a lid) for about half an hour until the fruit has softened. Take the spice bag out and sieve the fruit mixture to remove the seeds and skins.

Return the fruit mixture to the pan and add the sugar. Bring to the boil, stirring then boil furiously for about 8-10 minutes until the mixture becomes thick.

Pour into clean bottles and seal. This will keep for two weeks in the fridge or longer if you use properly sterilised and sealed bottles.

Samhain – 31st October-1st November

This has got to be what I would think is quite possibly the most celebrated pagan holiday. I love this time of the year – autumn is my favourite season with the crisp fresh air first thing in the morning and the colour of the trees. It is the end of summer and the third and final harvest of the year, a time when the veil between the worlds is at its thinnest; a time to celebrate the lives of those who have passed and to remember and honour our ancestors. Oh… and eat lots of sweets. Samhain is a good time to look back over the past year and let go of that which did not serve you and look forward to the year ahead. It is also an excellent time to work with your divination skills.

Aside from all the Samhain goodies that will give us all a sugar overdose, foods for this season make me think of big hearty casseroles, home baked bread and stick-to-your-ribs puddings.

Autumn is a fabulous time of the year to go out for a walk and although there isn't a huge amount to be found in the hedgerows at this time of the year you might be lucky enough to bag yourself nettles, sorrel, cow parsley, horseradish, crab apples, juniper berries, rosehips, sloes, chestnuts, walnuts and wild mushrooms.

Veggies that are in season in October/November: artichokes, aubergines, beetroot, borlotti beans, broccoli, Brussels sprouts, cabbage, carrots, cauliflower, celeriac, celery, chicory, courgettes, cucumber, endive, fennel, French beans, garlic, leeks, onions, parsnips, peas, peppers, chillies, potatoes, pumpkins, squash, radish, runner beans, spinach, swede, sweetcorn, tomatoes, turnips and watercress.

October/November seasonal fruits are: apples, blackberries, blackcurrants, damsons, greengages, grapes, medlars, melons, peaches, nectarines, pears, quince, raspberries and rhubarb.

Vampire's Blood (OK... Blackberry Cordial)

This is a yummy sweet syrup with spices and optional alcohol. Delicious cold with water over ice or made with hot water for a warming drink, it can also be poured over ice cream or steamed puddings.

Ingredients:
500g/17 ½ oz blackberries
500g/17 ½ oz sugar
2-3 tablespoons water
Optional – 6 tablespoons brandy

Method:
You will need a large jar or heatproof jug, pop the blackberries and the water into it. Pour half the sugar on top of the fruit. Stand the jar in a saucepan of hot water, bring to the boil and simmer for 1½ hours (keep an eye on the water level, don't let it boil out). Then strain the contents of the jar into a large saucepan squishing all the fruit through a sieve. Add in the rest of the sugar and bring the mixture back to the boil, stirring all the time. Once the sugar has dissolved keep stirring and boiling for a further five minutes. Remove it from the heat and allow it to cool. You may have to skim a little from the top of the mixture. You can now add in 6

tablespoons of brandy if you wish, giving it a good stir. Pour it into clean jars and put the lids on.

Magic of the ingredients:
Blackberries – Protection, healing, money
Sugar – Love and to make life sweet
Water – Emotions, release, purification

Chapattis

Now these might not be the most obvious choice for Samhain, but they are brilliant if you are having a party to celebrate as they can be made ahead and reheated or even frozen and reheated just before you need them. They work brilliantly with a great big pot of homemade curry, chilli or even savoury dips. They are also ridiculously easy to make. I use atta flour, which you can get from Asian supermarkets, but wholemeal flour works just as well.

Ingredients:
175g/ 6 oz atta or wholemeal flour plus extra for dusting
Good pinch of salt
110ml/4 fl oz water
1 teaspoon vegetable oil

Method:
Sift the flour and the salt into a large bowl. Add the water gradually (you might not need it all) and mix to a soft dough then knead in the teaspoon of vegetable oil.

Knead the dough on a lightly floured surface for about 5 minutes, until it is smooth. I do this process in the food mixer with a dough hook fitted. Place it in a lightly oiled bowl and cover with a tea towel, leave it to rest for about 20 minutes.

Take small pieces of the dough (walnut size) one at a time and roll them out on a floured surface; try to roll them as thin as you can.

Heat a non-stick frying pan – I have found that I don't need to use any oil as the non-stick coating does the job, but you may want to add a tiny amount.

Cooking each chapatti one at a time, place it in the hot pan over a medium heat for probably not even a minute – you will need to watch these as they cook fast! The chapatti will start to bubble, when it does turn it over and cook on the other side for a further 30 seconds.

You can keep them warm by wrapping them in a tea towel while you cook the rest of the batch.

Magic of the ingredients:
Flour – Prosperity, stability
Water – Emotions, release, purification
Salt – Purification, protection, cleansing

The Winter Solstice/Yule – 20th-23rd December

The shortest day and the longest night, it is from this day onwards that we start to get a little bit more sunlight each day. The Oak King and the Holly King fight, with the Oak King winning this time to reign over the waxing period of the year until the summer solstice, when they fight once more. It is a time for family, friends, get-togethers, feasting and celebrating.

We probably all over-eat at this time of the year. I like to think of it as fuel to help keep my body warm… The scents and tastes at Yule are amazing with cinnamon and cloves being my favourites, just the smell of mince pies baking in the oven sums up this season for me.

When you take a stroll after Yule dinner, keep an eye out for nettles, cow parsley, crab apples, juniper berries, rosehips, chestnuts and wild mushrooms.

Seasonal vegetables for December: Jerusalem artichokes, beetroot, borlotti beans, broccoli, Brussels sprouts, cabbage, carrots, cauliflower, celeriac, celery, endive, greens, leeks, lettuce, onions, parsnips, potatoes, pumpkin, squash, radish, spinach, swede, turnips and watercress.

The seasonal fruits for December: apples, pears, quince and forced rhubarb.

Coriander Cookies

These are brilliant for winter solstice rituals as they have the sun energy heat from the coriander seeds and they are sun shaped! The cookies are soft and spongy on the inside and crisp on the outside.

Ingredients:
150g/5 oz sugar
110g/3 ½ oz butter or margarine (room temperature)
1 egg
275g/9 ½ oz plain (all-purpose) flour
½ teaspoon baking powder/soda
Pinch of salt
1 teaspoon ground coriander

Method:
Beat the sugar and butter together until light and fluffy. Add in the egg. Mix in the flour, coriander, salt and baking powder and mix until just combined.

Drop tablespoonfuls of the mixture onto a baking sheet lined with baking parchment paper.

Bake at 350F/Gas 4/180C for about 12/15 minutes (or just until it starts to turn golden around the edges).

Magic of the ingredients:
Coriander – Healing, love
Butter – Spirituality
Egg – Healing, protection, love, fertility
Salt – Protection, purification, cleansing
Sugar – Love and to make life sweet

Festive Tea

Ingredients:
4 cloves
Pinch of ground nutmeg
Pinch of ground ginger
Pinch of ground cinnamon
Herbal fruit tea bag (raspberry or apple works well)
Boiling water
Teaspoon of honey

Method:
Pop all of the ingredients except the tea bag into a saucepan and bring to the boil then turn off the heat and drop in the tea bag. Allow it to steep for about 5 minutes then pour into a cup and drink while you eat a coriander cookie or a mince pie.

Magic of the ingredients:
Cloves – Protection, love, money, exorcism
Nutmeg – Luck, money, health
Ginger – Power, success, money, love
Cinnamon – Success, healing, power, love, protection
Honey – To make life sweet

Imbolc – 2nd February
This is a festival of light to celebrate the coming spring, new beginnings, purification, renewal and a time when the air is full of potential, ideas and fertility. It is the time of year when animals have given birth to their new offspring or are just about to so. Milk and dairy products are a key ingredient in a lot of Imbolc recipes, but any kind of fresh and light vegetables are as well, along with fish and lots of herbs and spices.

As you venture out into the wilds to breathe in the first signs of fresh spring air you might find chickweed, nettles, cow parsley, primroses, juniper berries and chestnuts in the hedgerows to add to your dinner table.

Seasonal veggies for January/February: artichokes, beetroot, broccoli, Brussels sprouts, cabbage, carrots, celeriac, celery, endive, greens, leeks, lettuce, onions, parsnips, potatoes, radish, spinach, swede, turnips and watercress.

The fruits in season for January/February are apples, pears and forced rhubarb.

Chai Tea Cup Cakes

Ingredients:
250g/9 oz self raising flour
½ teaspoon bicarbonate of soda
250g/9 oz sugar
½ teaspoon ground cloves
½ teaspoon ground cinnamon
½ teaspoon ground cardamom
250g/9oz butter
4 large eggs
3 tablespoons milk

For the icing:
300g/10 ½ oz butter
675g/23 ½ oz icing sugar
4 tablespoons milk
2 tablespoons Demerara sugar
1 teaspoon ground cinnamon
¼ teaspoon ground nutmeg
1 pinch ground cloves

Method:
Preheat the oven to 170C/375F/Gas 5.

Pop the flour, bicarb, sugar and spices into a large bowl. Add the butter and the eggs and beat for about a minute. Add the milk and whisk until the ingredients are all incorporated.

Fill 12 muffin cases with the mixture and bake in the oven for 20 minutes. Leave to cool.

For the icing, beat the butter until pale and smooth. Pop the icing sugar in a large bowl and gradually add the butter, beating well as you go. Add in the milk and beat until combined.

When the cakes are cool, ice the top and then mix the sugar with the spices and sprinkle over the top.

Magic of the ingredients:
Cloves – Protection, love, money, exorcism
Nutmeg – Luck, money, health
Cinnamon – Success, healing, power, love, protection
Cardamom – Love, lust
Sugar – To make life sweet, love
Eggs – Fertility, healing, protection, sex
Milk – Spirituality, love
Butter – Spirituality

Peppermint Fizz

Ingredients:
50g/1½ oz mint leaves
750ml/26 fl oz boiling water
2 tablespoons honey
3 tablespoons lemon juice
500ml/1 pint sparkling water

Method:
Wash the mint leaves (discard the stalks) and pop them in a jug, then pour over the boiling water. Leave this to steep for five minutes. Then add the honey and stir; leave to cool. Strain into another jug and pop in the refrigerator to chill. Just before you

serve add the lemon juice and sparkling water.

Magic of the ingredients:
Mint – Love, healing, psychic powers, purification
Honey – Love, happiness, spirituality, wisdom, purification, health
Lemon – Love, friendship, purification

Spring Equinox/Ostara – 20th-23rd March

The first day of spring and the festival of chocolate... or so it feels like, which is OK with me. Darkness and light are in balance and we now enter a time of renewal and rebirth, the earth is beginning to stir and starts to send out the first signs that spring has arrived. Celebrate fertility, abundance, new beginnings and put those plans and ideas into motion, get that manifesting on the move!

After your hearty Ostara lunch and all those chocolate eggs, you might like to stretch your legs in the countryside and look for Alexanders, chickweed, dandelion, fat hen, nettles, sorrel, watercress, wild rocket, cow parsley, meadowsweet, wild garlic and primroses.

Veggies that are in season during March: artichokes, purple sprouting, Brussels sprouts, cabbage, carrots, cauliflower, celeriac, endive, greens, leeks, lettuce, onions, parsnips, potatoes, swede and watercress.

Seasonal fruit is still a bit sparse but apples and forced rhubarb are good.

Lemon Curd Cupcakes

Ingredients:
250g/9 oz self raising flour
250g/9 oz sugar
½ teaspoon bicarbonate of soda

270g/9 ½ oz butter, softened
4 large eggs
Zest from 4 lemons
1 ½ tablespoons lemon juice
½ jar of lemon curd (approx 150g)

For the icing:
300g/10 ½ oz butter, softened
675g/23 ½ oz icing sugar
4 tablespoons lemon juice
1 tablespoon lemon curd
Extra lemon curd to decorate

Method:
Preheat the oven to 170C/375F/Gas 5.

Pop the dry ingredients into a large bowl. Add the butter, lemon juice, zest and the eggs and beat for about a minute. Add the milk and whisk until the ingredients are all incorporated.

Fill 12 muffin cases (or 24 fairy cake cases) with the mixture and bake in the oven for 20 minutes. Leave to cool.

For the icing, beat the butter until it is pale and smooth. Sift the icing sugar in a large bowl and gradually add the butter, beating well as you go. Gradually add in the lemon juice and beat until combined.

When the cakes are cool carefully cut off the top of each cake and pop in half a teaspoon of lemon curd, then put the top of the cake back on. Then ice each cake with the butter cream icing and I like to drizzle a little extra lemon curd onto the top of each one.

Magic of the ingredients:
Lemon – Love, friendship, purification
Sugar – To make life sweet, love
Eggs – Fertility, healing, protection, sex
Butter – Spirituality

Lemon Balm and Borage Refresher

This is a very nice drink full of the flavours of spring and the promise of summer.

Ingredients:
1 bottle of white wine
6 sprigs of lemon balm
6 borage flowers
½ tablespoon honey
6 slices of lemon
Bottle of sparkling water

Method:
Put the lemon balm and borage flowers into a jug and add the honey and lemon slices. Pour over the bottle of white wine, allow it to chill in the refrigerator then just before serving add sparkling water and ice to make it a nice long drink.

Magic of the ingredients:
Lemon – Love, friendship, purification
Honey – Love, happiness, spirituality, wisdom, purification, health
Lemon balm – Success, love, healing
Borage – Psychic powers, courage
Wine – Celebration!

Cooking with the Moon Cycle

The power of the moon is incredibly strong and affects our moods and emotions. By working with the cycles of the moon rather than against them, going with the flow so to speak can make our lives much easier. We can also tailor the foods we eat to the phases of the moon to tap into that power and to work with the rhythm of our bodies and emotions too.

Waxing Moon

For the waxing moon work with foods and menus that feed your soul, increase your strength and revitalise your spirit – bright, cheerful, spicy, exciting foods. Bring magic into your cooking for abundance, healing, love, creativity, manifesting and setting goals and dreams in motion.

Try using recipes on the waxing moon that include meat, fish or chicken, beans, grain and pasta, lots of vegetables and natural yogurts. Fill your recipes with lots of herbs and spices, the good ones that boost your immune system. For afters go for dairy-filled desserts or warming crumbles and fruit pies. This is an excellent time to try out new recipes and use ingredients that you haven't cooked with before; be daring!

Waxing moon: broccoli, carrots, corn, garlic, onion, sweet potato, peppers, colourful vegetables, meat, chicken, fish, grains, beans, dairy, fruits, basil, fennel, thyme, ginger, turmeric, honey.

Sweet Potato Bravas

This is my take on the traditional Spanish potato dish using sweet potatoes instead.

Ingredients:
Olive oil
1 onion, chopped

2 cloves garlic, crushed

1 tin chopped tomatoes

1 tablespoon tomato puree

2 teaspoons sweet paprika (or use smoked paprika if you prefer)

½ teaspoon chilli powder

½ teaspoon sugar

Salt & pepper

900g/31oz sweet potatoes

Method:

Fry the chopped onion in a little oil until softened (about 5 minutes) then add in the garlic, tomatoes, puree, paprika, chilli, sugar and salt and simmer for 10 minutes. Take off the heat and put to one side (this will keep overnight if necessary).

Preheat your oven to 200C/400F/Gas mark 6.

Cut the sweet potatoes into cubes and pop them into a roasting tin. Drizzle over enough oil to evenly coat the potatoes – the best way to do this is to get your hands in there and toss them around. Season them with salt and pepper. Roast the potatoes for 30-40 minutes until they are crisp.

Reheat the tomato sauce and pour over the sweet potatoes and serve.

Full Moon

On the full moon it is time to bring on the feast! Enjoy delicious and extravagant foods that celebrate the goddess in her mother aspect. Big rich foods full of flavour and all the good stuff that isn't healthy honour the goddess at this moment.

For the full moon pull out all the stops and make big hearty dishes of fish, eggs, pasta and rice. Make sure you throw in lots of warming spices. Bake potato dishes and cook with cabbage and cauliflower, adding herb-filled sauces and lots of chillies. To treat yourself afterwards go for sumptuous, decadent desserts filled with fruits, nuts and of course... cakes and chocolate.

Full moon: fish, eggs, pasta, sea food, all vegetables but particularly potato, cauliflower and cabbage, basil, tomatoes, mint, meat, thyme, oregano, tarragon, black pepper, chilli, garlic, cinnamon, fruits, nuts, cheese, cake and chocolate.

Pulled Pork

Ingredients:
A shoulder of pork
400ml/14 fl oz stock (vegetable or chicken)
A medium size piece of root ginger (about 2 inches long) sliced
4 star anise
Freshly ground black pepper
4 cloves of garlic, sliced

Method:
Set the oven on low (around Gas 2/150C/300F).

Place the piece of pork fat side up in a roasting tin, pour the stock and add all the other ingredients into the tin as well.

Cover the tin loosely with tin foil.

Pop in the oven and leave it for a good 4 to 5 hours then test it to see how it is getting on (depending on the size of the joint it may take longer). If the meat comes away from the bone with a fork then it is ready, if not take the tin foil off and leave for another hour.

This dish is very forgiving, if left covered with the foil you can leave it in the oven all day (just keep an eye on it).

Once the meat is ready you can take it all from the bone – 'pulling' it with a fork or with your fingers. This can then be put in a roasting dish.

Strain the juices from the tin into a jug and pour the stock over the pulled meat – this keeps it moist. You can cover this with foil and leave it in the oven to keep warm until you are ready for it.

Waning Moon

On the waning moon it is time to eat up all those leftovers, work with what you have in the fridge or the cupboards. Try and choose lighter foods, perhaps even ones that cleanse your system. Keep it light and keep it fresh.

For the waning moon keep it simple, fresh and cleansing. Work with citrus fruits, fresh vegetables and herbs, fish, rice and beans. Soups are excellent to make on this phase of the moon and throw in plenty of garlic. Herbal teas are also brilliant for the waning moon. For dessert go for fresh fruit and yogurt.

Waning moon: all vegetables, pasta, salads, parsley, coriander, rosemary, soft fruit, rice, beans, fish, citrus fruit, dried fruits, greens, sage, lemon and mint.

Lavender and Lemon Chicken

Ingredients:
1 whole chicken, jointed
2 tablespoons dried lavender
4 tablespoons olive oil
4 tablespoons honey
3 sprigs thyme
Zest and juice of one lemon
Pinch salt

Method:
Crush the lavender and pop it into a bowl together with the oil, honey, thyme, lemon zest and juice and mix together.

Put the chicken joints in a large dish or container and pour the marinade over the top, making sure each piece of chicken is well coated – you will have to get your hands dirty for this part! Cover and leave to marinate for at least half an hour, but preferably a couple of hours.

Preheat the oven to 200C/400F/Gas mark 6.

Put the coated chicken and the juices into a roasting tin and sprinkle over with salt. Roast for 45 minutes, turning the chicken pieces halfway.

New Moon

On the new moon we welcome the dark goddess; this is a powerful phase of the moon and a time for inner work. It is suggested that this time is one of fasting, but I would recommend just keeping things light and healthy and make sure you drink plenty of fluids.

Seasons

Obviously the moon phases span the seasons so we will eat differently on a spring full moon than on a winter one.

> **Spring moons** – This is a season of new beginnings, growth and awakening so eat the foods that inspire you to connect with the energies of spring.
> **Summer moons** – Summer is a time for sitting outside and eating whether it is dinner in your back garden or a picnic on the beach. It is a time for celebrating life and all that we have.
> **Autumn moons** – Harvest time. We start to think about warming, hearty foods and giving thanks to the land for all that she has supplied us with.
> **Winter moons** – It's cold and dark (and probably wet) so eating with the moon phases at winter will involve foods that warm us, keep us strong and maintain our bodies through the winter season.

The moon for each month also has its own magical properties and energies, go with your intuition and how you feel and how the energies around you make you feel and cook accordingly.

Magical Food for Intent

Foods can be used for specific intents, we have all heard about the aphrodisiac power of oysters and the healing powers of homemade chicken soup, but you can add your own intent to any of your cooking. Use the lists below to give you an idea of what foods work for which intent or go with your own intuition.

Charge each item as you add it to the pot, visualising your desired outcome. You could also draw magical symbols in the air above the food to add even more power to it or even carve symbols into the food itself – such as a love heart into the side of an apple.

You can also increase your magical intent by working with colour magic either with the colour of the foods or by lighting a corresponding coloured candle before you start cooking. Go with your intuition about what colours work for what purpose, but here is a basic list to give you an idea:

Colour Magic

Black – Protection, ward negativity, remove hexes, spirit contact, truth, remove discord or confusion and binding for spell work.

Dark blue – The goddess, water elemental, truth, dreams, protection, change, meditation, healing.

Light blue – Psychic awareness, intuition, opportunity, understanding, safe journey, patience, tranquillity, ward depression, healing and health.

Brown – Endurance, houses and homes, uncertainties, influence friendships.

Green – Earth elemental, nature magic, luck, fertility, healing, balance, courage, work, prosperity, changing directions or attitudes.

Indigo – Meditation, spirit communication, karma workings, neutralize baneful magic, ward slander.

Lilac – Spiritual development, psychic growth, divination, otherworld.

Orange – The god, strength, healing, attracting things, vitality, adaptability, luck, encouragement, clearing the mind, justice, career goals, legal matters, selling, action, ambition, general success.

Pink – Honour, morality, friendships, emotional love, social ability, good will, caring, healing emotions, peace, affection, nurturing, romance and partnerships.

Purple – Power, spirit, spiritual development, intuition, ambition, healing, wisdom, progress, business, spirit communication, protection, occultism, self assurance.

Red – Fire elemental, strength, power, energy, health, vigour, enthusiasm, courage, passion, sexuality, vibrancy, survival, driving force.

White – Purity, protection, truth, meditation, peace, sincerity, justice and to ward doubt and fear.

Yellow – Air elemental, divination, clairvoyance, mental alertness, intellect, memory, prosperity, learning, changes, harmony, creativity, self promotion.

Magical Food – Fertility

If you are wanting to hear the patter of tiny feet then add some magical fertility foods to your diet. Obviously there are other things you need to do to make babies happen, but that's down to you! Don't think you can only eat these items if you want to get pregnant, it doesn't work like that and you need to always eat a balanced diet… it is all down to the intent, visualisation and charging the ingredients.

Foods for Fertility

Eggs, figs, grains, grapes, milk, nuts, pomegranate, poppy seeds, rice, sesame seeds, watercress.

Baked Egg Custard

Full of fertility with the eggs and milk, you could also add a layer of figs to the bottom of the dish for that added… oomph.

Ingredients for the.pastry:
225g/8oz plain (all-purpose) flour
Pinch of salt
115g/4oz cold butter, diced
3 tablespoons cold water

For the filling:
425ml/15 fl oz full fat milk
Pinch of salt
85g/3 oz sugar
2 medium eggs
3 medium egg yolks (you can use the whites to make meringues)
150ml/5 fl oz double cream
Freshly grated nutmeg

Method:
Preheat the oven to Gas 5/375F/190C.

To make the pastry add the cold butter and salt to the flour and mix with your fingertips until it resembles breadcrumbs – or pop it all in the food processor and whizz together. Using a fork, mix in the cold water one tablespoon at a time (you might not need all three) until the crumbs form into dough.

Roll out the pastry and line a 9 inch tart tin preferably with a removable base if you want to turn it out. Make sure there are no holes in your pastry, if there are patch them up with little bits of pastry scraps. Prick the pastry with a fork, line it with baking parchment and fill with baking beans (or dried pulses/uncooked rice). Pop it in the fridge for half an hour.

Bake the pastry case for 10 minutes then remove the baking parchment and the beans and bake for a further 10 minutes so that the pastry is no longer raw. Remove it from the oven. Turn the oven heat down to Gas 2/300F/150C.

Put the milk, salt and sugar into a saucepan over a medium heat and stir until the sugar has dissolved then bring to the boil and remove from the heat.

Put the eggs and egg yolks into a bowl and beat together, then slowly add in the hot milk, stirring as you go. Strain the mixture through a sieve into a jug. Mix in the cream and pour the mixture into the pastry case. Grate a sprinkling of nutmeg over the top and pop in the oven for 30-40 minutes until just set. Leave to cool in the tin.

Magical Food – Grounding

Feel a little bit spacey? Floating high as a kite? This can happen after working with energy, spell work or in ritual or just because… This is why we eat cake in our rituals… well one of the reasons anyway – because eating can help to ground your energy.

Foods for Grounding

Beans, carrots, cheese, chocolate, eggs, grains, meat, peanuts, potato, salt, sweet potato, tofu and, of course, I have to mention cake here…

Potato Bread

Yes I know it sounds weird, but the potato makes for a really soft lush bread and with all those grains and potatoes you will be so grounded you will feel like the earth itself.

Ingredients:
2 large floury potatoes (about 400g/14oz)
1 ½ teaspoons fast action dried yeast
370g/13oz strong white bread flour
1 ½ teaspoons salt
70ml/½ fl oz buttermilk (or natural yogurt)

Method:

Peel the potatoes, cut into chunks and boil in plenty of water until soft. Drain the potatoes, but save about 200ml (7fl oz) of the cooking water. Mash the potatoes until smooth.

Pop the flour and salt into a large bowl, sprinkle in the dried yeast, mashed potato, buttermilk and 100ml (3 ½ fl oz) of the potato water and mix together. You will probably need the other 100ml of potato water as well, but add this in gradually as you may not need it all to create a soft, moist dough.

Turn the dough onto a floured surface and knead for about five minutes. Then place the dough in an oiled bowl and cover with a tea towel, leave for two hours to prove.

Pre-heat your oven to Gas 7/425F/220C.

Lightly knead the dough again for a couple of minutes then shape into a circle. Place it on a floured baking sheet, cover with a tea towel and leave for a further half an hour to prove again.

Dust the top with a light flour and then pop in the oven for about 45 minutes.

Magical Food – Happiness and Peace

We lead such busy lives now that sometimes finding that sense of peace, balance and happiness is a bit of a trial. I love to cook and eat, in fact heading into the kitchen for me is a way to relax and feel happy. The foods in this section have the magical properties of allowing us to unwind, to chill out and just relax… take a deep breath in… and let it go… ahhhhhhh. Let go of that which does not serve you and release the things that you can do nothing about. Pour yourself a glass of wine (just the one), sit down, put your feet up and eat something that gives you pleasure. If you don't like any of the items on this list then avoid them because eating something you don't like will definitely not make you happy no matter how strong the magical properties.

Foods for Happiness and Peace

Apples, apricot, chocolate, cucumber, cumin, fish, honey, lentils, lettuce, marigold, marjoram, milk, olives, oregano, passion fruit, peach, pizza, raspberries, rose, saffron, wine.

Apple and Cider Cake

What's not to love about this cake? Delicious apples and yummy cider, it will make your heart sing.

Ingredients:
55g/2oz sultanas
150ml/5 fl oz dry cider
1 large cooking apple, peeled, cored and chopped
115g/4oz butter, softened
115g/4oz light muscovado sugar
2 eggs
225g/8oz plain (all-purpose) or wholemeal flour
1 teaspoon baking powder
1 teaspoon ground cinnamon
1 tablespoon Demerara sugar

Method:
Preheat the oven to Gas 5/375F/190C. Lightly grease and line an 8 inch cake tin.

Put the sultanas in a bowl and pour over the cider. Dice the apples into pieces about the same size as the sultanas and add them to the cider.

Cream together the butter and muscovado sugar until light and fluffy. Gradually beat in the eggs a little at a time.

Sift the flour, baking powder and cinnamon into the mixture and stir until combined. Fold in the flour and then the fruit and cider. Mix gently until all the ingredients are incorporated.

Spoon the mixture into your prepared tin, sprinkle the Demerara sugar over the top and bake for about 45/50 minutes.

Leave in the tin to cool for a few minutes then turn out onto a wire rack.

Magical Food – Healing and Health

We all know that a healthy balanced diet is the one to go for to maintain good health. I don't advocate crash diets, in fact I don't believe in diets as such at all. If you want to lose weight then change your habits, look at what you eat and the way you eat. Don't cut out a whole food group from your diet. All things in moderation. We all like to have a treat now and then and I am pretty sure we all deserve a cake once in a while (not a whole family size cake in one sitting obviously...). But we need the balance of protein, carbs, fats (good ones), vitamins and minerals to keep our bodies healthy and functioning properly. Eat up your vegetables, grains and fruits, but keep to a minimum processed food, salt and sugar. I am not a trained nutritionist... just use your common sense. If the diet reads 'lose a stone in two weeks' then you will probably be living on cabbage water for the whole two weeks and will make yourself fairly ill...

There are no magic wands to wave to cure all ills. I do advocate seeking holistic and spiritual treatments, reflexology worked absolute wonders for me, but... don't radically change your diet and never stop taking any kind of medication without the say so of your doctor.

I do believe healing comes from within. The mind is a powerful thing and we can manifest worries and stresses as physical conditions in our bodies... enter the holistic therapies to keep stress to a minimum and therefore reduce the physical illness.

Foods for Health and Healing

Almond, apples, Brussels sprouts, chicken, cider, cucumber, garlic, honey, lemon, olives, melon, mint, peach, pineapple, pumpkin, sage, tomato, walnuts.

Chicken and Sage Soup

Ingredients:
50g/2 oz butter
1 onion, chopped
1 tablespoon chopped sage or 1 teaspoon dried sage
450g/16 oz leeks, finely sliced
450g/16 oz potatoes, peeled and sliced
1 litre (1 ¾ pints) chicken stock
250g/9oz shredded cooked chicken

Method:
Melt the butter in a pan and add the onion and sage. Pop a lid on and sauté for about 10 minutes. Add the leeks and the potatoes, then top with enough stock to cover all the vegetables. Bring it to the boil and simmer for about half an hour.

If you like a thicker soup you can take a couple of cups of the soup out and blend it in a food processor then stir it back into the rest of the soup.

Stir in the cooked chicken, reheat and season to taste.

Magical Food – Love
Love doesn't just cover the romantic kind it also includes friendship and families. Just getting a group of friends or family together for a feast or just a pizza in front of the TV bring love into your home and your life, but you can add a little bit of magic if you tailor your food choices with the right intent.

Foods for Love
Anise, apple, apricot, avocado, banana, basil, beetroot, brazil nut, cardamom, chocolate (obviously!), cinnamon, cherry, chestnut, clove, coriander, fennel, fish, ginger, guava, honey, lemon, lime, mango, marjoram, milk, nectarine, orange, papaya, passion fruit, peach, peas, pineapple, pine nut, pistachio, poppy seeds, quince,

raspberry, rhubarb, rose, rosemary, strawberry, sugar, sweet potato, thyme, tomato, vanilla and wine!

Chocolate Truffles

I just had to go with chocolate for the intent of love and these are really easy to make and can be tailored to your own tastes by adding in your own flavourings.

Ingredients for the ganache:
250g/9oz dark chocolate, broken into pieces
20g/½ oz butter, diced
250ml/9 fl oz double (heavy) cream

For the coating:
250g/9oz dark chocolate, broken into pieces

Method:
What you are actually making here is a chocolate ganache, which can also be used to fill tarts and pies.

Heat the cream in a bowl over a pan of simmering water until the cream starts to simmer, keep an eye on it because you don't want it to boil. It just needs to be warm enough to melt the chocolate. When it starts to bubble around the edges remove the pan from the heat and add the chocolate and butter. Stir until the chocolate has melted and the ingredients are all combined.

At this point you can add in any flavouring such as:

3 tablespoons of black coffee
A teaspoon of vanilla extract
3 tablespoons of alcohol such as rum or whiskey

Pour the mixture into a baking tray lined with baking parchment and pop it in the fridge for half an hour to an hour. Keep an eye on it, you want it to set but not rock hard. You need to be able to mould it into shape.

Remove it from the fridge and, using a teaspoon, scoop out balls of the chocolate ganache then roll them in your palms to make perfect ball shapes (OK not really perfect, just roundish is good enough). Pop them on a tray lined with baking parchment and when they are all done put them back in the fridge for a further 15/20 minutes.

To make the coating put the second lot of chocolate pieces into a bowl over a pan of simmering water and stir until melted. You can do this stage in the microwave, but zap it for short bursts and keep checking because it is easy to burn.

Now you need to drop each chocolate ganache ball into the melted chocolate, roll it around then lift it out.

At this point you can keep it simple and set the truffles onto clean baking parchment to set or you can add extra such as crushed nuts, chocolate nibs, coloured sugar, salt flakes, edible flower petals, a dusting of cinnamon or be creative.

Rosemary Conserve

This can be used in the same way you would honey and can be made with other herbs such as borage, sage and thyme.

Ingredients:
500ml/1 pint rosemary sprigs
500ml/1 pint water
Juice 1 lemon
400g/1 lb sugar

Method:
Wash the rosemary sprigs and pop them into a saucepan with the water. Bring it to the boil and then simmer for five minutes. Take it off the heat and leave to cool. Strain the liquid back into the saucepan and add the lemon juice and sugar. Slowly heat and stir until the sugar dissolves, then boil rapidly for 6-7 minutes until

the syrup starts to thicken. Pour into warm dry jars and seal with lids when cold.

Magical Food – Luck

Need a bit of luck to come your way? You can add to your chances of winning the lottery… OK maybe not that lucky, but changing the tide of luck to your favour can be enhanced by eating foods that have lucky magical properties.

Foods for Luck

Bananas, beans, cabbage, coconut, coleslaw, green vegetables and fruit, hazelnuts, nutmeg, pancakes, rice, sauerkraut.

Coleslaw

Who would have thought the humble coleslaw was so full of luck? I love coleslaw, but not the usually disappointing shop-bought stuff; homemade coleslaw is a whole different realm. I prefer drier coleslaw, but if you like lots of mayo just keep adding a spoonful at a time until you get the consistency you like.

Ingredients:
½ of a whole white cabbage
½ of a whole red cabbage
5 carrots
225g/8 oz mayonnaise
1 tablespoon Dijon mustard
1 tablespoon sugar
2 tablespoons cider vinegar
1 teaspoon fennel seeds
½ teaspoon salt
½ teaspoon freshly ground black pepper

Method:
Finely slice both the cabbages and roughly grate the carrots.

Whisk together the mayonnaise, mustard, sugar, vinegar, fennel seeds, salt, and pepper. Pour the dressing over the vegetables and stir well.

Magical Food – Magical powers
Now these foods aren't going to make you fly on a broomstick or make sparks come out of your fingers, but they are high in magical properties and can give you that extra magical oomph.

Foods for Magical Powers
Chocolate (yay!), citrus fruits, coffee, dates, figs, honey, leeks, meat, pineapple, proteins, rum, salt, spicy food, tea, tofu.

Honey Scones
Honey to me is one of the most magical ingredients and can add a huge boost of magical powers... and of course you can't go wrong with scones especially with jam and cream...

Ingredients:
200g/8oz plain (all-purpose) flour
2 teaspoons baking powder
Pinch of salt
75g/3oz butter, softened
1 tablespoon light soft brown sugar
2 tablespoons honey
2-3 tablespoons milk

Method:
Preheat the oven to 200C/400F/Gas Mark 6.

Mix together the flour, baking powder and salt and rub in the butter. Add the sugar and mix together. Stir the honey into the milk and mix until it dissolves. Keep back a tablespoon of the milk and honey mix to brush over the top of the scones during baking and tip the rest into the flour mix. Mix to form a soft dough.

Shape the dough into a round and put it on a greased baking sheet, score the top with a knife to divide it into eight wedges.

Bake in the oven for 15-20 minutes.

Remove from the oven and brush the reserved honey and milk mix over the top then pop it back into the oven for a further 5-10 minutes.

Remove from the oven and serve warm with butter, or at room temperature with jam and cream.

Magical Food – Prosperity

I am guessing that we could all do with a little bit of extra cash every now and then, usually more now than then. There are a lot of spells you can work to keep the cash coming in and I have covered these before. A lot of it involves visualisation and convincing yourself and the universe that you deserve it. Negative thoughts won't bring the money in. Know that you are worthy.

When you eat foods that correspond to money and prosperity as with all of the intents, visualisation is the key, as you eat see yourself comfortable and secure. I think it also helps to pay it forward and give something back. I regularly have a clear out and give bags of clothes or toys to charity and I always drop some coins into collection boxes when I pass them, if you can't afford money then how about giving some of your time to a local volunteer charity?

Foods for Prosperity

Almond, aubergine (eggplant), basil, banana, beans, black-berries, cabbage, cinnamon, clove, dill, figs, ginger, grains, grapes, lettuce, maple syrup, milk, nuts, parsley, pears, peas, pineapple, pomegranate, pumpkin, rice, salt, seeds, spinach, tea, tomato.

Gingerbread

This is a sticky heady spicy moist cake that keeps for a good while and freezes well. It is nice to have with a cup of coffee or warm with custard.

Ingredients:
225g/8oz butter
225g/8oz light muscovado sugar
225g/8oz gold syrup (or corn syrup)
225g/8oz black treacle
225g/8oz self raising flour
225g/8oz wholemeal self raising flour
4 level teaspoons ground ginger
1 teaspoon cinnamon
2 large eggs
300ml (½ pint) milk

Method:
Pre-heat your oven to 160F/Gas 3/325C.

Grease a 12 x 9 inch baking or roasting tin and line it with baking parchment.

Put the butter, sugar, golden syrup and treacle into a saucepan and heat gently until the mixture has melted and combined. Stir occasionally and then allow it to cool slightly.

Pop the flours and spices into a large bowl. Beat the eggs and the milk together. Pour the cooled butter and syrup mixture into the flour and add the egg and milk mixture. Beat together until smooth. Pour into the prepared tin.

Bake in the oven for about 50 minutes.

Allow to cool in the tin for a few minutes then turn out onto a wire rack.

Blackberry Syrup

This can be used as a drink diluted with hot or cold water or on top of ice cream or sponge puddings. It keeps well in the refrigerator for several months.

Ingredients:
500g/1lb blackberries
500g/1lb sugar
2-3 tablespoons water

Method:
You will need a large jar with a lid. Pop all the blackberries into the jar with the water then add half the sugar. Stand the jar in a saucepan of hot water, bring to the boil and simmer for one and a half hours. Strain the contents of the jar into a clean saucepan. Make sure you give the mixture a squish with the back of a spoon to get all the juice through the sieve. Add the rest of the sugar to the pan with the juice. Bring it to the boil and stir until all the sugar has dissolved, then boil for a further five minutes. You may need to skim the top. Allow it to cool a little then pour it into clean bottles. Once cold, put lids on the bottles and store.

Magical Food – Protection

However careful we are we can always use a little bit of extra protection, whether it is personal to us and our bodies and emotions or whether it is bringing in protection to our homes and families. I do believe the best protection we can give ourselves is the psychic shield; a bubble visualisation of protection around our bodies, while for our houses a good sprinkling of salt around the boundary and regular smudging should do the trick. However, if we eat foods on a regular basis that have protective energies it can't do anything but help add to our personal armour even if all we do is breathe over annoying people after we have eaten a big chunk of garlic bread...

Foods for Protection

Almonds, artichoke, basil, bay, black pepper, blueberries, broccoli, Brussels sprouts, cabbage, cauliflower, cayenne, chillies, chives, clove, corn, cranberries, curries, eggs, fennel, garlic, horseradish, leeks, mango, marigold, meat, mustard, olive oil, onions, oranges, paprika, parsley, peppers, pineapple, plum, potato, quince, radish, raspberries, rice, rhubarb, rosemary, rum, sesame seeds, soy sauce, spicy foods, sunflower seeds, tofu, tomatoes, vinegar, walnut, watercress.

Baked Chicken Curry

This looks complicated because of the long list of ingredients, but it really isn't. It can easily be made vegetarian by exchanging the chicken for your favourite vegetable. Butternut squash works well.

Ingredients:
2 teaspoons cumin seeds
2 teaspoons coriander seeds
1 teaspoon fennel seeds
2 teaspoons ground turmeric
1 large onion, roughly chopped
3 large garlic cloves, crushed
1 green chilli, roughly chopped
1 piece of root ginger (about 2 inches long), roughly chopped
4 tablespoons vegetable oil
1 chicken, jointed into 6 pieces, or 6 skin-on, bone-in chicken
  pieces
400g/14 oz tin of tomatoes
400ml/14 fl oz tin of coconut milk
Sea salt and freshly ground black pepper

Method:
Toast the cumin, coriander and fennel seeds in a dry frying pan

for a minute or so then grind them to a powder and mix in the turmeric.

Put the onion, garlic, chilli and ginger into a food processor and blitz to a paste.

Heat a couple of tablespoons of oil in a pan over a medium heat and add the chicken pieces. Season them with salt and pepper and sauté until they are a nice brown colour. Transfer them to a large roasting dish (skin side up).

Reduce the heat and add the spice mix and onion paste, stirring continuously fry for 3 or 4 minutes. You can add a little more oil if it needs it.

Tip the tomatoes and the coconut milk into a bowl and mix together. If you prefer a smoother sauce you can blitz them with a blender. Pour the mixture into the frying pan and simmer, stirring continuously. Season with salt and pepper then pour the sauce over the chicken pieces making sure they are all well coated, but also make sure there isn't loads of sauce sitting on top of the chicken.

Bake in a pre heated oven 180C/350F/Gas mark 4 for one hour. Be sure to turn and baste the chicken pieces once or twice during cooking.

Horseradish Sauce
This works well for protection and purification. The root of the horseradish will need washing and peeling then left to dry for a bit. Use the coarse side of the grater.

Ingredients:
3 tablespoons grated horseradish
¼ teaspoon mustard powder
3 tablespoons double (heavy) cream

Method:
Mix all the ingredients together.

Magical Food – Purification

Do you ever get that feeling that something is not right, that things are just a little bit out of whack? It is at that point that I smudge my house and renew my witches' bottles, but it can also help to give our bodies a bit of purification too. Get rid of the negative energy and replace it with new, fresh and positive vibes in the form of lovely food.

Foods for Purification

Bay, beer (not too many!), black pepper, coconut, edible flowers, fruit juices, grapefruit, honey, horseradish, lemon, limes, melon, mint, onions, oranges, salt, shellfish, soup, steamed vegetables, thyme, turmeric, vinegar, water, yeast recipes.

Onion Soup

This soup always reminds us of our visits to Paris, sitting outside a cafe in the Montmartre eating big bowls of steaming hot onion soup with so much cheese on the croutons it should really be called cheese soup.

Ingredients:
2 tablespoons vegetable oil
6 medium onions thinly sliced
1 tablespoons (level) plain (all purpose) flour
A dash of Worcestershire sauce
1.5 litres/52 fl oz of stock, beef works best but you could use vegetable
1 pinch salt
1 teaspoons black pepper

Although not in keeping with the purification theme you can add cheese-topped croutons.

Ingredients:
15g cheese, grated
French bread stick sliced and toasted

Method:
In a large non-stick saucepan heat the oil and very slowly sauté onions over a medium-high heat until they are golden brown, about 40 minutes. Stir occasionally to make sure the onions don't stick to pan.

Add the flour and mix to combine. Slowly pour in the stock, stirring constantly and add the Worcestershire sauce. Bring to the boil. Cover, reduce the heat and simmer for 20 minutes. Season to taste.

Sprinkle the cheese over the French bread, grill until bubbling. Ladle the soup into six bowls and top with bread.

Magical Food – Sex

Bring on the oysters and the strawberries dipped in chocolate, its *va va voom* time! Food has always (as far as I can tell) been used to seduce and add that extra sparkle to our love lives. I am not a personal lover of oysters or caviar, but it seems to do the trick for a lot of people. Add in a little bit of champagne and the romance is on.

Please don't use sex magic to lure someone who is unaware of what is going on; it is not only going against their free will and chances are it won't work anyway… but the universe has a habit of sorting things out when people are up to no good. Use these foods to create a sexy and romantic meal for you and your loved one.

Foods for Sex

Blackberries, brandy, caraway seeds, cardamom, carrots, caviar, celery, champagne, chocolate, chowder, coffee, cognac, coriander, eggs, figs, fish, honey, liquorice, mangos, mint, nuts, olives, parsley, parsnip, rice, rum, seeds, shellfish, sweet potato, truffles (fungi variety and chocolate ones!), vanilla (don't overdo the alcohol though!).

Chilli and Chocolate Tart

It had to be chocolate didn't it? Add to that the spicy kick of chilli and *va va voom*...

Ingredients for the pastry:
200g/7oz plain (all-purpose) flour
Pinch of salt
100g/3 ½ oz cold butter, diced
½ -1 egg, beaten

For the filling:
175ml/6 fl oz double (heavy) cream
125ml/4 fl oz milk
125g/4 ½ oz milk chocolate, chopped
175g/6oz dark chocolate, chopped
2 eggs, beaten
½ teaspoon chilli flakes

Method:
Preheat the oven to 180C/350F/Gas 4.

To make the pastry, place the flour, salt and butter in a bowl and mix with your fingertips until it resembles breadcrumbs (or whizz in the food processor) then add half the egg and start to bring the mixture together to form dough. If you need more egg add a little at a time. When you have a nice dough, wrap it in Clingfilm and pop in the fridge for about half an hour.

Put your dough on a floured surface, roll it out and use it to line a 9 inch tart tin.

Line your pastry case with baking parchment, fill it with baking beans and bake for 15 to 20 minutes then remove it from the oven.

Heat the cream and milk in a saucepan to boiling point then take it off the heat and stir in the chocolate until it melts. Allow it to cool for a few minutes then stir in the eggs and chilli flakes.

Pour the chocolate mixture into the pastry case and bake in the oven for 15-20 minutes until set.

Remove it from the oven and allow it to cool.

Magical Food – Spirituality and Psychic Skills

I am not talking about religion here, but finding your inner peace and your connection to the divine – whatever divinity it may be – finding your place and your faith.

The foods in this list may help you to find that connection or to strengthen your psychic abilities and divination skills, but more importantly hopefully they will help you find your inner sense of peace and spiritual connection.

Foods for Psychic Development

Aubergine (eggplant), banana, bay, butter (the real stuff not margarine), celery, cinnamon, coconut, corn, courgette (zucchini), dandelion, dates, eggs, fish, fruit juice, honey, lemon grass, mace, milk, mint, mushrooms, nutmeg, olives and olive oil, rose, saffron, shellfish, squash, thyme, tofu, vegetable soup, wine, yogurt.

Saffron Bread

This bread dates back to the late 15th century, but was originally a savoury bread. Later on the sugar and spices were added. Eat it with jam and cream or toasted with lots of butter.

Ingredients:
Pinch of saffron strands
300ml/10 ½ fl oz milk
2 teaspoons dried fast action yeast

500g/1 lb 2oz plain (all purpose) flour

Pinch freshly grated nutmeg

1 teaspoon ground cinnamon

½ teaspoon salt

170g/6 oz cold butter, diced

85g/3 oz sugar

170g/6oz sultanas (or a mixture of sultanas and chopped dried apricots)

85g/3oz chopped mixed peel

Method:

Crush the saffron to a powder and set aside.

Put the milk into a pan and bring it to just below boiling point, then remove from the heat and add the saffron. Leave it to infuse for half an hour. Then sprinkle the yeast in and carefully mix, leave for a further 10 minutes.

Sift the flour, salt and spices into a bowl and add the butter. Mix with your fingertips until it resembles breadcrumbs (or whizz in the food processor). Mix in the sugar, sultanas and peel. Add the milk/yeast mix and them bring together to form a soft dough.

Turn the dough onto a floured surface and knead for about five minutes. Place it in a greased bowl and cover with a cloth for two hours to prove.

Preheat the oven to 190C/375F/Gas mark 5. Lightly grease a 9 inch cake tin and line the bottom with baking parchment.

Turn the dough out and knead it again for a couple of minutes then place it in the cake tin. Cover it again and leave for a further one hour.

Bake the bread in the oven for one hour, then remove and leave to cool slightly before turning it out onto a wire rack.

Basic All-Purpose Recipes

You can pack a huge amount of magical energy very simply by making an herb oil, vinegar or butter. Here I have given some basic recipes but experiment! Leave them for a couple of weeks for the flavours of the herbs to infuse. I have also added some basic recipes such as biscuits, cake and pizza because they also work very well as magical energy 'carriers' that can be personalised for your own intent.

Herbal Oil

You will need:
A sterile bottle or jar with a lid
500ml/1 pint extra virgin olive oil
½ cup fresh herbs or 5 sprigs

Method:
Pop your herbs into the jar and pour the oil over the top then put the lid on – how simple is that!

If you want to speed up the process you can heat the oil and herbs in a saucepan over a low heat for about 10 minutes then pour into the sterile bottle and seal.

Herbal Vinegar

You will need:
A sterile bottle or jar with a lid
500ml/1 pint vinegar
2 cups or 2 good handfuls fresh herbs

Method:
The choice of vinegar is up to you, whether you use brown,

white wine, red or cider. Pop the herbs in your jar. If they are large leafed herbs you might want to chop them first. Pour over the vinegar then seal. Herbal vinegar benefits from being left to stand on a window sill in the sunlight. Depending on where you store your vinegar to infuse and how much sunlight it gets, it will take between 1 to 3 weeks to infuse properly. When it is ready, strain it and pour it into a sterile bottle or jar.

Herbal Butter

You will need:
250g/9 oz butter, softened
5 tablespoons chopped fresh herbs
1 tablespoon lemon juice

Method:
Mix all the ingredients together and pop in a tub or wrap and keep in the refrigerator. It will keep for up to two weeks.

Syrup
You can make a syrup base using sugar or honey.

For a sugar syrup base you will need:
Equal quantities of sugar and water.

Method:
Bring the water to the boil and simmer until the sugar has all dissolved.

For a honey syrup base you will need:
Equal quantities of honey and water.

Method:
Simmer the honey and water over a medium heat, stirring until the honey dissolves into the water.

You can add all sorts of edible flowers, herbs and fruit juices to your basic syrup to bring the magical intent in. If you are using fruit juice you can add it when you simmer the water and honey or sugar. For herbs or flowers, add them to the cooled syrup and leave overnight to steep, then strain. Keep your syrups in sealed bottles.

Sweet Biscuits
Use this base recipe and add in any herbs or spices that match your intent.

> *Ingredients:*
> 125g/4oz butter
> 125g/4oz sugar
> 250g/8oz plain (all-purpose) flour
> 1 egg, beaten

Method:
Pre-heat your oven to 375F, Gas 5, 190C.

Cream the butter and sugar together until pale and fluffy. Add in the egg and then sift in the flour and mix until combined to form a firm dough. Now add in your herbs or spices, visualising your intent and desired outcome as you stir them in.

Leave the dough to rest in the fridge for about an hour if you can as it will make it easier to handle.

Roll your dough out on a lightly floured surface and cut the dough into shapes either with cookie cutters or go freestyle… Pop the shapes onto a greased and floured baking tray and bake in the oven for about 10 minutes.

Leave the biscuits to cool on a wire rack.

Sponge Cake
Use this sponge recipe as a blank canvas, adding in different spices, fruits or even herbs. Tray bakes are brilliant as they are simple to

make and excellent to cut up and use for rituals or celebrations.

Ingredients:
225g/8oz butter, softened
225g/8oz sugar
275g/10oz self raising flour
2 level teaspoons baking powder
4 large eggs
4 tablespoons milk

Method:
Pre-heat your oven to 180F/Gas 4/350F. Grease and line the base of a 12 x 9 inch baking or roasting tin.

This is an all-in-one recipe so all you have to do is pop all the ingredients into a large bowl and whisk them together until combined. If you are adding spices, fruit or herbs, stir them into the mixture at this stage.

Pour the mixture into your prepared tin and bake in the oven for 35-40 minutes. Leave the cake to cool in the tin then cut it into pieces.

Pizza

A pizza base is a perfect background to add in all sorts of wonderful magical ingredients if you fancy something savoury rather than sweet (personally I would have both...).

You can buy packets of pizza mix that you just add water to, but it is really easy to make.

Ingredients:
300g/10 ½ oz strong bread flour
7g (2 level teaspoons) fast action dried yeast
1 teaspoon salt
3 tablespoons olive oil
175ml/6 fl oz warm water

Method:

Pre-heat your oven to 240C/475F/Gas 9.

Combine the flour, salt and yeast in a bowl and then gradually add the oil and water, mixing together to form a soft dough. It will be slightly sticky.

Dump the dough onto a floured surface and knead for about 10 minutes (or 5 minutes in a mixer with a dough hook).

Divide the dough into 3 equal pieces then roll them out nice and thin. Place them on greased baking sheets, then add your toppings.

You can go with the traditional tomato sauce, but I like to use a white béchamel sauce instead.

Once you have added your toppings bake them in the oven for 8-10 minutes

Crystallising
Edible flower petals and herb leaves can be crystallised quite effectively.

Ingredients:
1 egg white
1 tablespoon water
Sugar
A fine paintbrush

Method:
Put the egg white and water into a bowl and stir to mix. Paint each side of the flower or herb leaf very thinly with the egg mix, making sure you don't use too much. Then sprinkle over a light dusting of sugar. Dry them and then they can be stored in a tin, laid onto sheets of greaseproof paper.

Herb Bag
These are really useful for adding the flavour and magical properties of herbs to your cooking, but without having to fish out

bay leaves at the end or having big pieces of herb floating around.

The proper chefy name for it is *'bouquet garni'* a French term meaning 'garnished bouquet'.

If the herbs you are using are fairly robust, such as rosemary and sage, you can tie the herbs together in a little bundle with some twine (make sure it isn't coloured twine that will leech the colour into your cooking!). Otherwise you can use a small muslin bag – pop the herbs of your choice in and tie up the top. This can then simply be dropped into your casserole, soup or whatever you are making – just remember to take it out before you serve the dish...

You can even charge the ingredients as you add them to the bag and say a little chant or blessing as you pop it into the pot.

A traditional *bouquet garni* might have bay, thyme, parsley, celery and leek with maybe some peppercorns too, but go with your intuition, what works with your dish and your magical intent.

Poppets, Charms and Offerings

You can use food as poppets or to make charms and offerings.

A potato or any kind of root vegetable makes a good poppet or, if you are feeling creative, then make a gingerbread man/woman or a figure out of bread dough.

Make a bread or a salt dough and add protective herbs then create a symbol or shape with the dough. Once baked you can varnish it and hang it in your home.

Charms can be made from bread dough or biscuits – just work your choice of herbs or spices into the dough as you make them. You could even shape the dough. For example, if you were making a handfasting loaf you could shape it into a heart for love.

Offerings for deities or the fae can be as simple as a drop of honey or milk in your garden (the fae especially love this) or make small cookies and leave them in the woods as an offering to deity.

Magical Food Spells

You can incorporate food into lots of spells; most people have food of some sort during ritual anyway, so bring it into your spell work.

Most of us at one time or another eat magical food without even knowing it. We eat specific foods at celebrations such as wedding or handfasting cake, a bit of boozy fruit cake at Yule and chocolate eggs at Ostara. We have probably all blown out the candles on a birthday cake and made a wish – all magical foods.

When you are cooking with an intent in mind it is so simple to work that into your food, whether it is via visualisation or adding in herbs and spices that correspond with your intent.

Below is a very traditional type of bottle spell. It is basically a jar or even a box that has a sweet liquid inside. You then add your magical ingredients, such as connections to the person if you are directing it towards a particular individual, herbs and maybe a written charm on a piece of paper. This is all topped off by dressing a candle with a corresponding conjure oil and then the candle is burnt on top of the jar. You can use honey as the sweet liquid or you can use granulated or cubed sugar as well just as effectively, but if you use granulated or cubed sugar you might want to dissolve it in water first to make a syrup.

A Honey Jar Spell to Sweeten a Person
If there is a person who needs their personality sweetened, or you want to make them like you more, or you perhaps want a raise in your job and need to 'sweeten up' your boss, this is the trick to work.

What you need:
A jar with a metal lid
Honey, syrup or sugar

Slip of paper and a pencil
Personal items such as hair or nail clippings
A candle
Dressing oil

Method:
Fill your jar with your chosen sweetener. Then write the person's name on the slip of paper; write it out three times, each time on a separate line. Then turn the slip of paper around clockwise a quarter turn and write your own name three times, each time on a separate line. What you should have now is your names crossing each other.

On the space around the names, write down your wish; be specific. Write it around the edge of the paper so that it forms a circle around the names. This needs to be written without taking your pencil or pen off the paper and needs to be written in a continuous flow without any spaces. Make sure you join up the first and last words so that they form a circle. When you have done that you can go back and dot any 'i's and cross any 't's if you wish.

Once that is done fold the paper towards you and then speak your wish out loud. Turn the paper and fold it again, keep doing this – turning and folding towards you – to bring your wish to you until you can't fold it any more. If you want to add herbs or personal items to the spell, add them inside the piece of paper before you fold it, you could add rose petals for love, a clove for friendship or a piece of hair. Be creative and go with what feels right for you.

When you are ready, you will need to eat three spoonfuls of the honey, syrup or sugar. As you eat each one, state your wish out loud. Then put the folded piece of paper into the jar and close the lid.

Next dress your candle with an oil of your choice. You can also correspond the colour of your candle with the intent of your working. Then put the candle on top of the jar lid. You might need to pop a few drops of melted candle wax on the lid first to fix the candle in place.

Light the candle and let it burn fully. You don't have to burn it all in one go, but make sure you eventually burn it right out. Burn it on a Monday, Wednesday and Friday until it is done. You can keep this spell working by adding a new candle to the lid each time one burns right out until your desire is fulfilled.

The honey jar spell will work very well without the addition of a candle, but I find it adds more oomph to the trick and gets things working faster and is more powerful in the long run. It is a personal choice.

An Oven Blessing
Probably one of the main features in a kitchen is the oven, historically it would have been the centre, the hearth and heart of the home so it makes sense (to me anyway) to give your oven a blessing. Be nice to your appliances and they will be nice to you…

What you will need:
A baking sheet
Some flour
Pinch salt

Method:
Sprinkle a small amount of flour onto the baking sheet and then sprinkle over the salt. Flour is excellent to use because it represents not only earth where it grew, but it also the other elements it needed in order to grow – water from the rain, fire from the sun and air. The salt just brings a bit of protection in with it.

Now you can make a pattern in the flour/salt mix whether you want to draw a spiral to symbolise life, a goddess symbol, a sun or moon or something else, go with your intuition and draw something in the flour mix with your finger.

Now add your energy to the flour mix by visualising a strong white light bringing peace, love, protection, stability and harmony. Ask for your food and home to be blessed.

Pop the tray into the oven, but don't switch it on, just leave it be until you next need to use the oven.

Apple Spell for a Happy Home
This spell will bring peace and love into your home and family.

What you need:
An apple and peeler
Three cloves
Pinch of thyme

Method:
Pop the cloves and the thyme into one hand and hold your other hand over the top then say out loud all the names of the people within your household including your pets. Ask the universe, the divine, the goddess, the angels (whatever you prefer to work with) to bless your home and bring balance and peace to your household and everyone in it.

Then peel the apple, trying to keep the peel in one long strip. Pop the cloves and the thyme inside the apple peel (the wet side so they stick) then roll the apple peel up into a tight spiral bundle and tie it with oven-proof string.

Pop the bundle into the oven and bake on a medium heat for about an hour. Not only will it make the house smell nice, but it will also fill your home with positive magical energy. When it is baked, take it out and pop it on a shelf in the kitchen to continue working its magic.

Sugar Jar Spell for a New Home
If you are looking to move house this sugar jar spell could help things along.

Find a photo of the house you want to move into or a picture of your ideal home if you haven't found one yet and write your family name over it. Place the photo into a jam jar or a mason jar.

You will need enough sugar to fill the jar. Add to it a pinch of cinnamon for success, a pinch of allspice for money and a pinch of cloves for money and positive energy. Then you will need a house key, just an old one, doesn't need to be specific.

Pour the sugar mix into the jar on top of the photo and then stick the key into the sugar as if you were putting it into a lock. Turn the key as if you were opening a door. As you turn the key, visualise you and your family moving into the house of your dreams. You can even say your wish out loud or make up a chant. Turn the key three times.

Once at day, taste a little of the sugar or add it to your coffee (or tea). As you do this, repeat your visualisation and your chant if you used one.

Repeat the key turning and the sugar tasting every day until you get your house.

You will probably need to replace the sugar occasionally to keep it topped up.

Once you are in your new home use the sugar to bake a cake or some cookies and share them with those who need a financial boost.

Take the photo of the house that you used and bury it in the grounds of your new home (or in a pot plant if you don't have a garden).

Edible Flowers

Some flowers can be eaten and some even taste nice! Be careful to check you have identified the plant correctly and don't ever use flowers that have been picked by the roadside or anywhere near fields that have been sprayed with pesticide.

Bergamot – Prosperity, clarity and success
Borage – Grounding, success, support, humility
Calendula (marigold) – Healing, lifting your spirits
Carnation petals – Healing, protection
Chamomile – Peace, protection, prosperity
Chrysanthemum petals – Protection
Clover – Love, protection, prosperity
Cornflower – All purpose
Daisy – Love, lust
Elderflower – Protection, fertility, money
Garlic flowers – Protection, healing
Jasmine – Money, love, dreams
Lavender – Love, protection, purification, happiness, peace
Lilac – Protection
Nasturtium petals – Wealth, passion, love
Pansy – Passion, love
Rose petals – Protection, love, healing
Sunflower petals – Growth, negativity

Magical Food Correspondences

I have used traditional magical property correspondences as well as my own personal ones, but always go with your intuition about what feels right to you. There is no right or wrong correspondence.

Almond
(Prunus dulcis)
Use almond oil to anoint or add to floor washes; add it to your incense blends for any of the magical properties mentioned.

Use almonds in handfasting rituals or spell work for joining people together.

Pop almond nuts or leaves in your pocket, medicine pouches or witches bottles to bring money in. Keep an almond in your pocket to lead you to treasure (probably not the kind buried by pirates, but treasure comes in all guises).

Almond wood makes wonderful love magic wands.

This food is said to stimulate your intuition and insight along with activating your third eye.

An old story tells of Phyllis who died of grief after her lover Demophoon left her. The gods turned her into a barren almond tree. When Demophoon returned he saw the tree and put his arms around it. As he did so, the tree burst into flower and leaf thus symbolising true love even after death.

Almond magical properties:
Love, prosperity, treasure, intuition, psychic powers, passion.
Ruling planet – Mercury
Element – Air
Gender – Masculine

Apple

(Pyrus spp)

The apple is a very magical fruit right throughout history.

Cut an apple in half across its centre and you will reveal a five-pointed star.

The tree produces a lovely wood to use for wand making and is a favourite of witches, especially with its link to the autumn equinox and Samhain.

Apples are excellent to use in any love spell workings or recipes, but also for healing.

Eating an apple is said to open a portal into the other realms and allows us to gain clarity and knowledge.

Apples are also symbolic of abundance.

Apples are often connected with the mysteries of Avalon so work well in any incense blends or spell workings to connect with Avalonian deities. Apples are also considered the food of the dead so they are excellent to use in spirit work. Or maybe bake an apple pie and dedicate it to Avalon and eat to honour your ancestors.

Pick an apple and carve the initials of the one you desire and your own initials into the fruit, then bury the apple in the ground to set your spell into motion.

Peel an apple in one long continuous piece then drop the peel. The letter that it forms is the initial of your true love's name.

Apple magical properties:
Love, healing, clarity, knowledge, abundance, spirit work.
Ruling planet – Venus
Element – Water
Gender – Feminine

Apricot

(Prunus armeniaca)

The apricot is an orange coloured fruit from a small tree and looks very similar to a peach… but smaller. The skin is soft and downy like that of a peach… or a baby's bottom…

You can use all parts in magical work – the fruit flesh, stone (kernel), flowers and leaves.

The garden of paradise tended by Hesperides contained 'golden apples', which some believe were not apples at all but apricots or peaches that promised eternal youth.

It is an excellent fruit to use in love recipes whether you eat the fruit or just use the juice in spell work, lotions or potions.

Eating the fruit is said to bring about a sweet disposition.

The dried leaves and flowers can be used in medicine pouches and bottles and the apricot stone can be carried to bring love to you.

The apricot brings with it a very strong feminine energy, but still a gentle spiritual and floaty ahhhhh kind of energy, definitely one for romance and passion and even a little bit of an aphrodisiac quality…

Apricot Magical Properties:
Peace, love, passion, romance.
Ruling planet – Venus
Element – Water
Gender – Feminine

Artichoke (Globe)
(Cynara cardunculus/scolymus)
My dad used to grow globe artichokes on his allotment. We would sometimes eat them and they are quite nice. They are a bit fiddly, but quite often they would be left to dry for my mum to use in flower arrangements. They are part of the thistle family, which explains why the flower does resemble a thistle flower.

You can eat the buds, the lower fleshy part and the base or 'heart'. You can cook and pull off each of the bracts and dip them in melted butter or cook the hearts and use them in salads, dips and quiches.

It is a brilliant ingredient for any protection spell work or to disperse/dispel negative energies and can also be used for personal growth workings.

Eating the artichoke bottom was once said to cause a stimulating effect on young women so they were warned not to eat them lest they gave in to temptation...

Similar to the thistle, the artichoke is also good for bringing the magical energy of courage and strength to any spell work.

The cardunculous variety has hermaphroditic flowers, so male and female aspects are both included, which gives it a nice balance of energies.

The smaller flowers when dried on the stalk make unusual wands.

Artichoke Magical Properties:
Protection, growth, passion, strength, courage.
Ruling planet – Mars
Element – Fire
Gender – Masculine/Feminine

Asparagus
(Asparagus officinalis)
A spring vegetable and a flowering perennial, we all know about the asparagus being an aphrodisiac and this is quite possibly because, let's face it... this vegetable looks like a willy.

Eat asparagus when it is fresh and young as the older it gets the less tender and more woody it becomes. Stir fry, grill, steam – it cooks very quickly and is nice dipped into poached eggs, hollandaise sauce or melted butter. Although the asparagus generally available is green you can also get white asparagus. It is the same plant, but the growing technique uses soil to cover the plant as it grows so that it effectively blanches the colour, creating white asparagus.

There is a downside to eating asparagus because bizarrely it does make your wee smell and it is quite a distinctive odour. Victorian ladies could identify the smell and the husband would be accused of being unfaithful ... knowing that asparagus had been eaten as an aphrodisiac and presumably they hadn't been the ones receiving the benefits...

The ancient Greeks ate asparagus for cleansing and healing.

Asparagus Magical Properties:
Passion, sex, cleansing, healing.
Ruling planet – Mars, Jupiter
Element – Fire
Gender – Masculine (well it wouldn't be anything else really would it?)

Avocado
(Persea americana)
This is the fruit of a flowering tree, sometimes called an alligator pear (much better name than avocado in my opinion). Each fruit contains a large round and very hard stone/seed. It is an ancient fruit and evidence of its existence dates back millions of years.

The avocado is said to promote beauty, which probably links in with avocado oil being used in lots of different cosmetics and beauty regimes.

The Aztecs ate the fruit as an aphrodisiac and also believed it to be a fruit of fertility – so much so that during harvesting they would not allow their young daughters outside...

So if you want a boost of love, passion and *ooh la la*... avocado is your magical choice...

Avocado Magical Properties:
Beauty, passion, love, fertility.
Ruling planet – Venus
Element – Earth
Gender – Feminine

Aubergine (Eggplant)
(Solanum melongena)

There can't be many vegetables that are such a beautiful dark purple in colour as the aubergine (also called eggplant). Related to the tomato and the potato, the aubergine is also a member of the nightshade family.

It is a bit of a tricky vegetable to use in magical workings such as medicine bags... it would have to be a very large bag, but you could dry the flowers or the leaves for such a use.

Associated with money, wealth and prosperity, the aubergine makes wonderful dishes for the accumulation of the pennies... and hopefully the folding currency too.

Aubergine (Eggplant) Magical Properties:
Prosperity, wealth.
Ruling planet – Jupiter
Element – Earth
Gender – Feminine

Baking Powder/Soda

Bringing with it the element of air, baking powder raises energy and gives an added oomph to your magical workings.

Baking Powder/Soda Magical Properties:
Energy, magic.
Element – Air

Banana
(Musa spp.)

You don't really need me to tell you what a banana is... it grows in clusters at the top of trees. I did wonder for a long time where the banana 'seeds' were and how it propagated, in case you are dying to know... the mummy banana meets a daddy banana... OK maybe not... actually it promulgates through ground shoots.

The plant produces a pseudo stem, which creates a banana heart, which develops into the cluster of bananas. After 'fruiting' the stem dies, but as it will have already created more ground shoots the life cycle continues.

The story of how baby bananas are made gives us the magical properties of life cycles and prosperity.

The bananas also grow facing the sky, which gives us the magical property of spirituality.

And yes we have another vegetable/fruit that is shaped like a willy, so it has very masculine energies.

Banana Magical Properties:
Prosperity, spirituality.
Ruling planet – Mars
Element – Air
Gender – Masculine

Barley

(Hordeum vulgare L)
A member of the grass family this grain is a super healthy, high fibre, high protein whole grain. Used in making barley malt, which is a key ingredient of beer (got your attention now?), it is also used in cattle feed. But it is yummy, tastes a bit like brown rice and can be added to all sorts of recipes.

Barley is one of the oldest grains believed to have been cultivated, around 10,000 BC.

Barley is most definitely a Lughnasadh (Lammas) grain.

It is a Venus plant so can be used in all sorts of love magical workings and recipes.

Sprinkle barley around the boundary of your property to provide protection.

Tie barley straw around a pebble and throw it into a river or the sea to take away any illness or pain.

Associated with the heart chakra, barley can help ease

emotional issues and turn them into positive energy.

Barley is also very good for grounding.

Barley Magical Properties:
Love, healing, grounding, protection.
Ruling planet – Venus
Element – Earth
Gender – Feminine

Basil
(Ocimum basilicum)

This is a well known herb that I love to use in cooking and team with tomato and mozzarella in a salad. It is only an annual though so won't survive outside during the winter. I keep a pot on my kitchen windowsill. It has soft tender stems with bright green shiny oval leaves that are highly scented. There are all sorts of different types of basil – Greek, lemon, Thai, purple, cinnamon and I have a very unusual smelling basil mint at the moment. One of the folk names for basil is 'witch's herb'.

Basilicum is from the Latin word basilisk, a snake-like creature that was said to cause madness and even death. Basil was eaten to ward against any such attack, so far I haven't been killed by a basilisk, but I am not so sure about the madness...

It was said that witches used to drink basil juice before flying on their broomsticks; personally I would just add it to an incense blend to aid in astral projection...

Folklore states that basil seeds need be planted whilst hurling swear words about, this apparently dates back to the idea that swearing brought protection with it and caused any evil demons to be confused, allowing the plant to grow profusely.

Plant a pot of basil and look after it when it is growing really well. Give it to someone that you love, this will encourage love between you.

Pop a basil leaf in your purse to keep money coming in.

Rub a basil leaf on your skin to create a 'love attraction' perfume.

Write something that you wish to banish from your life on a basil leaf and leave it out in the sun to dry, then grind it up and burn it. As you burn it, it will release the negative energy. You could also write a personal goal on a basil leaf and eat it.

Use basil in protection powders and exorcism and purification incense blends. It is also useful to pop in an incense blend to bring peace to a household after an argument. The same magical properties could be achieved by adding basil to your meals.

Warning – be careful about over indulging on basil while pregnant.

Basil Magical Properties:
Wealth, money, prosperity, love, exorcism, protection, happiness, peace.
Ruling planet – Mars
Element – Fire
Gender – Masculine

Bay
(Laurus nobilis)
The bay grows as a tree – the laurel, but it does grow slowly so it does very well in pots if you have a small garden. You can pick the bay leaves all year round.

Bay probably gets its association with psychic powers from being used in incense at the Delphic oracle.

Add bay to any spell work to give it a bit of a power boost.

Used dried bay leaves in incense blends to purify, cleanse, protect and bless your home and also to increase your spiritual and magical connections when in ritual.

Bay can also be used in pouches and powders to help increase your creativity and inspiration. Place a bay leaf under your pillow to bring insightful dreams. Write a wish on a bay leaf and bury it, burn it or send it off into the wind for it to come true.

Hang a bundle of bay leaves (or if you are feeling creative make a bay wreath) above your door to bring protection to your home. Also carry a bay leaf with you for personal protection and strength.

Use bay leaves in your cooking so that it can impart all of these magical properties, but remember to remove the bay leaf from the dish before eating as it is a bit tough.

Bay Magical Properties:
Protection, purification, strength, power, healing, creativity, spirituality, psychic powers.
Ruling planet – Sun
Element – Fire
Gender – Masculine

Bean
(Phaseolus spp)
There are lots of different types of green bean – green bean, runner bean, French bean, garden bean etc.

This is a climbing annual plant with white and sometimes red flowers (depending on the variety) grown for the 'fruit' of the plant... the green beans.

Also included in this group are the beans we use just the 'seeds' from, such a pinto bean, kidney bean and broad bean.

Basically a whole load of beans...

In ancient Egypt and Greece beans were thought to contain the souls of the dead (quite small souls obviously) and you were therefore not allowed to eat them or destroy the plants.

Linked to the ancestors, the humble bean can be used in workings for wisdom and divination.

Shelling beans from their pods was said to bring prosperity your way, so use them for money workings.

Apparently if a single woman finds a bean pod with nine beans inside she should hang it over her doorway... the next eligible man who walks through will become her husband (presumably whether he likes the idea or not...).

Beans Magical Properties:
Wisdom, divination, prosperity.
Ruling planet – Mercury
Element – Air
Gender – Masculine

Beef

Meat from cattle (cows and steers). Most meats are generally classed as being associated with the element of fire, but I think any animal that grazes has an earth connection too.

Beef being a red meat is said to give aggressive and excitable qualities... but anyone who has eaten a huge roast beef dinner on a Sunday lunch time could argue with that assumption.

Beef is sacred to the Egyptian goddess Hathor.

The female cow brings lunar qualities, but the bull is definitely a sun kinda guy, bringing with him power and fertility.

Beef Magical Properties:
Power, fertility.
Element – Fire, Earth
Gender – Masculine

Beer

Beer is made from grain and water (and other stuff obviously), so it brings together the elements of earth and water.

Apparently on Samhain Celtic warriors held contests to see who could drink the most beer, believing that the course of action would make them immortal... just like any Saturday night down the pub then...

Don't tell the blokes, but according to historical evidence... women invented beer.

Beer is a good liquid to use to purify the body, just add a little to your bath water or drink a small amount... yes I did say 'small' amount.

The Egyptians believed that dreaming of beer was a good omen.

Beer has long been used as a ritual offering and makes a nice ritual drink when in circle.

Beer Magical Properties:
Dreams, purification, offerings.
Ruling planet – Mars
Element – Fire
Gender – Masculine (got to be really?)

Beetroot
(Beta vulgaris)
Part of the *Amaranthaceae* family with many varieties, the most well known is the beetroot, but chard and sugar beet are also included and probably the best ever named vegetable, the mangelwurzel, which is used for animal feed.

The beetroot we are most familiar with has a beautiful deep red/purple colour although you can get golden varieties too. The juice makes a useful magical ingredient if you are squeamish and don't want to use blood in any of your workings... not that I do on a regular basis, I'm just saying!

The beetroot is one of passion and symbolises love and beauty and is sacred to the Greek goddess of love, Aphrodite.

The beetroot corresponds to the heart chakra.

Use beetroot juice to write your love spells.

The beetroot has a really earthy flavour, so works well for grounding too.

They are particularly messy to prepare and will stain your

hands red. If you want to use the property of beetroot in your magical workings such as medicine bags etc you can dry very thin slices of the beets and then grind into a powder.

Mixed with chocolate, beetroot actually makes a very nice cake.

Beetroot Magical Properties:
Passion, love, beauty, grounding.
Ruling planet – Saturn
Element – Earth
Gender – Feminine

Blackberries
(Rubus fruticosus)
Blackberries or bramble berries grow in the wild as well as being cultivated. It is a perennial that grows like a loony with pretty white flowers followed by green fruit that go red then black... oh and the whole plant is covered in nasty spikes.

The blackberry is a bit of a magical all-rounder when it comes to the elements as the berries are ruled by the element of earth, the leaves ruled by Venus and water and the thorns are Aries and fire.

Blackberries promote prosperity, I assume because of the speed the plant grows and the amount of fruit produced.

The spikes on the plant give it the magical energy of protection and if you can brave the scratches blackberry branches make a good protective wreath for your home.

The amount of berries produced and the amount of seeds contained in the fruit also gives it the magical energy of fertility.

Eat them or bake them into pies and cakes to utilise the magical properties, but if you want to use the power of black-berry in medicine pouches and incense blends, use the dried leaf or root ... it's less messy...

Folklore says that passing under an archway of brambles will cure all manner of afflictions including pimples and boils.

Blackberries are also a fruit of the faerie world.

Folklore also states that blackberries will protect you against spirits and vampires... I have not tried this, having never met a vampire (well not knowingly anyway).

Dreaming of blackberries can mean loss or sorrow and if you are pricked by a blackberry thorn in your dream it means your enemies are conspiring against you.

Blackberries Magical Properties:
Prosperity, protection, fertility, faerie.
Ruling planet – Venus
Element – Water, Fire, Earth
Gender – Feminine

Black Pepper
(Piper nigrum)
We probably all use black pepper on our food, but it has amazing magical properties too.

The black pepper corns we are familiar with are the berries (red in colour) that are picked before they are fully ripe from the pepper tree, which can grow up to 20 feet tall. The seeds are then dried in the sun and turn black.

Black pepper corns are brilliant in protection sachets, bottles and amulets; they also help to release jealous thoughts and feelings.

It is also useful in powders to protect the boundaries of your property and to repel any negative energy. Mix ground black pepper corns with paprika and chilli powder to really bring in the protection... this also makes a very hot spicy dry rub for use on chicken or steak.

Peppercorns also work well in personal amulets and pouches to bring out your inner strength and give you that hot peppery roar of confidence when you need it.

Used medicinally as a gargle, black pepper can paralyse the tongue so it makes sense to me to use the peppercorns in workings to stop people gossiping about you.

If you have a visitor at your house who you don't want to return, just after they have left you can throw a pinch of black pepper mixed with salt after them. This should deter them from coming back.

Black Pepper Magical Properties:

Protection, exorcism, jealousy, negativity, strength, confidence, gossip.

Ruling planet – Mars

Element – Fire

Gender – Masculine

Blueberries

(Vaccinium Cyanococcus)

The blueberry plant is a perennial flowering plant that produces indigo blue berries.

The blueberry is a totally hippy fruit that brings with it the energies of peace, calm, acceptance and protection... yeah man...

Blueberries are especially useful in workings and spells to prevent a psychic attack.

It is another fruit that is good for fertility workings and also to add a bit of *va va voom* to your sex life.

Eat the fruit fresh or dry the berries and the leaves to use in medicine pouches and incense blends... oh and muffins, of course, coz blueberry muffins are delicious.

Blueberries Magical Properties:

Calm, peace, protection, passion, fertility.

Ruling planet – Moon

Element – Earth, Water

Gender – Feminine

Brazil nut
(Bertholletia excelsa)

Brazil nuts are produced on huge – and I mean huge (up to 160ft) – trees that can live for hundreds of years producing large capsules of 'fruit' that contain up to 24 brazil nut seeds in each one.

Pop a few Brazil nuts into a blender with some olive oil, give it a whizz and you have Brazil nut butter.

The Brazil nut is a luuuurve nut so use it in any magical workings or recipes for that love thang.

Carry a Brazil nut with you to bring love and good luck for relationships and also keep one with you to bring money your way.

Brazil nut Magical Properties:
Love, prosperity.
Ruling planet – Venus
Element – Earth
Gender – Masculine

Bread

Bread is one of the first baked food products, apparently dating back to the Neolithic era (about 8,000 years ago). Leavened bread was made in Egypt around 4000BC when the basic diet was bread, onions and beer… a bloke's diet then…

Bread is sacred to the goddess Isis.

Bread is a basic mixture of flour, water, salt and yeast, to which all sorts of extra ingredients can be added. Yeast is 'alive' so a loaf carries the energy of life within it.

Don't leave your loaf lying upside down though… it will attract negative energies.

The bread will also carry with it the particular energies of the grain that was used to make it whether it is wheat, barley, rye etc.

Bread is excellent for use in ritual to honour deity and to ground after energy work.

Bread Magical Properties:
Depends on the grain used, all breads are good for offerings and grounding.
Element – Earth
Gender – Feminine

Broccoli
(Brassica oleracea)
From the cabbage family, the word broccoli means 'flowering crest of a cabbage'… which sounds much grander than just plain ol' broccoli… The one we are most familiar with is *calabrese broccoli,* but personally I love purple sprouting broccoli.

When your children won't eat their broccoli you can remind them that broccoli was considered to be a very valuable vegetable by the Roman Empire…

The Romans believed that broccoli increased your strength and leadership qualities… so make sure you eat up all your greens.

Broccoli is sacred to the god Jupiter.

Eat it to bring in personal protection energies.

Broccoli Magical Properties:
Strength, protection.
Ruling planet – Moon
Element – Water
Gender – Feminine

Brussels Sprouts
(Brassica oleracea)
The Brussels sprout is another one from the *Brassica oleracea* family and they look like teeny tiny cabbages. They are a definite love or hate vegetable. I have to admit it… I love them. They are especially good in risotto or raw sliced thinly in coleslaw or sproutslaw as we call it in our house.

The tale of the humble Brussels sprout is one of stability, endurance and protection so eat 'em up for all of those magical energies.

Brussels Sprouts Magical Properties:
Stability, endurance, protection.
Ruling planet – Moon
Element – Water
Gender – Feminine

Butter

Not the imitation margarine stuff, we are talking about the real deal here, proper full fat thick creamy butter.

Apparently the Mesopotamians ate butter around 3500BC. It was considered a sacred and spiritual food and quite magical.

Add a bit of butter to a recipe to help soothe a troubled relationship or smooth over an argument.

The fae are quite partial to butter so it makes a good offering to them.

Butter Magical Properties:
Peace, spirituality, faerie.
Ruling planet – Moon
Element – Earth
Gender – Feminine

Cabbage
(Brassica oleracea/var.)

This is a white, green or purple leafy vegetable that comes in all sorts of varieties. It is good sliced raw or cooked… but not boiled to death because apart from making the house smell horrid it tastes like last week's laundry.

The cabbage is supposedly one of the oldest foods known to man.

Eating cabbage will help stimulate your base chakra.

Medieval folklore suggests that newlyweds were given cabbage soup the first day into their marriage to ensure that their love stayed strong... not much of a honeymoon feast!

Cabbage is also said to be a powerful bringer of fertility... you have been warned... watch out for those cabbage patch babies...

Irish folklore says that blindfolded girls were sent out to pull up the first cabbage they could find. If there was a lot of soil around the root then they would marry a wealthy man; unfortunately if the root was free from soil they would wed a poor man. The taste of the cabbage would also predict the disposition of their husband to be – sweet or sour... I am not sure what it meant if the cabbage had a caterpillar in it...

Cabbage is a brilliant food to use on the full moon and also eat for personal protection.

Cook cabbage and eat to bring prosperity your way.

Cabbage Magical Properties:
Moon magic, protection, prosperity, fertility, love.
Ruling planet – Moon
Element – Water
Gender – Feminine

Cake
Well I just had to mention cake didn't I?

Cakes have featured throughout history for centuries and have often been used in ritual, for celebrations or rites of passage. Cakes were offered to the gods or eaten at ceremonies to appease them or encourage good harvests or even to ensure that the sun rose the next day... Personally I don't need any excuse to eat cake... we eat cake during ritual after the energy work to help us ground us and we eat it at our workshops for breakfast... and elevenses... and lunch... and a snack...

A cake is one of the simplest recipes to enchant with magical energy and carries the energies of all the usual ingredients such as flour, eggs, butter and sugar, but can then be given a boost by adding in other flavours.

Soul cakes were made on All Souls Day and Mexicans make special cakes for *Dia de los Muertos* (Day of the Dead) and moon cakes are eaten at Chinese lunar festivals.

The ancient Greeks left cakes at crossroads in order to appease the goddess Hecate, sometimes apparently with a single candle in so that she could find it in the dark... the forerunner of the birthday cake perhaps?

Cake also makes people happy...

Cake Magical Properties:
Happiness, ritual, rites of passage, offerings, celebration, grounding.
Element – Earth
Gender – Feminine

Cardamom
(Elettaria cardamomum)
Lovely warm spice that not only brings heat to your food, but also to your passion. The seeds are the parts used and these are collected from the plant just before they ripen.

With the warmth of the spice it works well for lust and love, but is also stimulating to the body and mind, bringing clarity of thought and uplift to the spirit.

Add cardamom seeds to the food or drink you intend to share with a partner. It will add passion to your relationship.

Carry cardamom seeds with you to attract love. Add the pods to incense blends to use in your home to bring protection and love to the house.

Cardamom Magical Properties:
Love, passion, clarity, uplifting, protection.

Ruling planet – Venus, Mars
Element – Water
Gender – Feminine

Carrot
(Daucus carota)

Did you know the original carrot was purple and didn't taste very nice? Talented gardeners developed it into the orange coloured sweet tasting veggie we are familiar with today.

During the Middle Ages physicians prescribed carrots for all sorts of afflictions including syphilis and dog bites.

There is heap loads of masculine energy in the carrot and also the magical properties of fertility.

The ancient Greeks made a love potion from carrots, which was believed to endow men with passion while compelling women to become submissive.

The Roman emperor Caligula was once believed to have fed the senate a banquet of carrot dishes in the hope that it would produce a 'delightful orgy for his viewing pleasure'.

Wow, the humble carrot holds some tantalising magical secrets... who knew?

I will never view the carrot in the same light again...

Carrot Magical Properties:
Clarity, fertility, passion.
Ruling planet – Mars
Element – Fire
Gender – Masculine

Cashew
(Anacardium occidentale)

The cashew tree is a tropical evergreen tree that produces the cashew apple and the cashew nut. The cashew nut that we are all familiar with is produced at the end of the cashew fruit. The fruit can be used to make juice drink. The cashew nut is literally born from the 'womb' of the cashew apple so it brings a good punch of feminine energy with it.

Eat cashew nuts to give you an extra energy boost.

Add cashew nuts to your spell workings to increase prosperity.

Cashew Magical Properties:
Prosperity, energy.
Ruling planet – Sun
Element – Fire, Earth
Gender – Feminine

Cauliflower
(Brassica oleracea)
Another one from the *Brassica* family, the cauliflower is an annual plant with a white 'flowering' head.

It has a very feminine energy ruled by the moon, the cauliflower is excellent for moon magic and spell work for the emotions.

Eat cauliflower to bring in personal protection.

Cauliflower Magical Properties:
Emotions, moon magic, protection.
Ruling planet – Moon
Element – Water
Gender – Feminine

Caviar
Not my own personal idea of perfection on a plate and I think it is a very acquired taste, but basically it is teeny tiny fish eggs from the sturgeon.

The Romans believed sturgeon to be the most amazing tasting fish and honoured it by serving it on a platter scattered with roses.

Caviar is from a sea creature and ruled by the moon and the element of water, so is most definitely a food for the emotions.

It is also one of the foods considered to be an aphrodisiac, 'Here darlin' have yourself some fish eggs'…

Caviar Magical Properties:
Emotions, passion.
Ruling planet – Moon
Element – Water
Gender – Feminine

Celery

(Apium graveolens var. dulce)
The stalks, leaves and seeds of the celery can be eaten, but it is very much a love or hate kind of vegetable as the flavour is quite strong. The stalks are delicious dipped in salt and I like to add sliced celery to casseroles. It also makes a good stock base together with carrots and onions.

Celery brings with it the magical properties of passion and clarity… an interesting combination…

The stalks are best used in recipes and workings for passion and lust while the seeds can be used for concentration and mental clarity.

The seeds are also good to use to bring calm and peace.

Celery Magical Properties:
Clarity, passion, peace.
Ruling planet – Mercury
Element – Fire, Water, Air
Gender – Masculine

Cheese

Oh so many cheese varieties and made from all kinds of different milk and all so delicious! It is an ancient food (I am not talking about that old lump of cheddar stuck in the back of your fridge). Pots used for separating curds have been found dating back to around 6000BC.

Cheese is sacred to the Greek god Apollo and symbolises everything coming together and a successful outcome.

Add cheese to your cooking because... well because cheese just makes most recipes better, but also because it will bring positive energy in.

It is brilliant to use in ritual for feasting and if you are feeling inventive you can even cut a hard cheese such as cheddar into crescent moon shapes... seriously if you have the time to do that you need to get out more...

It seems that the old wives tale of cheese giving you nightmares stems back to the stories about hags appearing in the night and being 'hag ridden' i.e. having nightmares. A lot of these stories included the consumption of cheese, the hag offering the unsuspecting person cheese and then turning them into beasts of burden.

Cheese Magical Properties:
Success, happiness.
Ruling planet –Saturn
Element – Earth, Air
Gender – Masculine

Cherry

(Prunus avium/cerasus)

This is a deciduous tree with absolutely beautiful blossom in spring followed by delicious cherries – *P. avium* is the sweet or wild cherry and *P. cerasus* is the sour cherry sometimes used in cooking.

The cherry has always seemed very feminine to me with the stone held inside the 'womb' of the actual fruit so it makes sense to me that it is a good fruit to use not only for love magic, but also for fertility.

Use the wood of the cherry tree, stones or the dried blossoms in love incense blends.

The stones have long been used for divination purposes. I can remember as a child doing the 'tinker, tailor, soldier, sailor, rich man, poor man, beggar man, thief' rhyme with my cherry stones to see who I was going to marry... I don't recall any of the stones ever saying 'drummer'...

You can also use cherry juice as a substitute for blood in rituals or workings.

I also like to use cherry blossom or stones in magical workings for new beginnings drawing on the spring energy.

Cherry Magical Properties:
Love, fertility, divination, beginnings.
Ruling planet – Venus
Element – Water, Air
Gender – Feminine

Chestnut (Sweet)

(Castanea var.)

A deciduous tree, the sweet chestnut produces spiky seed pods that hold the 'fruit' inside. It is not to be confused with the horse chestnut, which looks similar but is fairly inedible although is good for playing games of conkers...

We have been eating chestnuts since around 2000BC apparently and the armies of Alexander the Great were noted as favouring them.

The nut has a very strong masculine energy and the tree is often associated with Zeus.

Eat chestnuts to encourage fertility and carry them with you to aid in conceiving.

Pop a few chestnuts around the house to bring in abundance and prosperity.

Eat chestnuts to encourage success and strength.

Chestnut Magical Properties:
Strength, success, prosperity, abundance, fertility.
Ruling planet – Jupiter
Element – Fire
Gender – Masculine

Chicken

Funny, feathered, pecky things… I really don't have to describe a chicken to you do I?

Said to promote well being, chicken soup has become very well known for its healing and restorative properties.

Chicken was often sacrificed to the gods by the Romans and that is still done in some religious practices around the world today, so the chicken symbolises personal sacrifice too.

Grain was scattered on the ground and chickens allowed to peck at it. The patterns left were then read to tell the future.

Chicken bones make an excellent divination set.

Chicken bones also make useful additions to money drawing and luck pouches.

Eggs are a symbol of fertility so it makes sense to me that the chicken itself also corresponds to fertility.

I also believe the bones of an animal take on some of its totem animal properties so with a chicken that would be fertility and sacrifice.

Chicken Magical Properties:
Healing, divination, prosperity, luck, fertility.
Element – Fire
Gender – feminine

Chillies

(capsicum)
Such a huge variety of these spicy morsels and in quite a fabulous array of colours too. Eat them, use them in workings or string

them up and use as decorations…

Apparently Christopher Columbus referred to them as 'peppers' because of the spicy black pepper taste.

I like to add a pinch of chilli powder to any magical workings that need a bit of an energy or power boost, the hotter the chilli powder the bigger the magical oomph that it carries.

The chilli carries with it a huge power punch of creative energy too.

Sprinkle chilli powder into medicine pouches and witches' bottles to bring in protection. This also works around the boundary of your home.

Pop a dried chilli or two underneath your pillow to spice up your love life or enjoy a spicy meal together.

Chilli works really well in any hex breaking spells as well.

The ruling planet of chillies is the fiery Mars and they are associated with the god Mars as well so they carry the warrior energy within.

Chillies Magical Properties:
Creativity, energy, power, protection, passion, hex breaking.
Ruling planet – Mars
Element – Fire
Gender – Masculine

Chives

(Allium schoenoprasum)
A perennial plant that is part of the onion family, the long slender green 'tubes' have a very oniony taste and the purple flowers are not only pretty, but edible too.

They were often used in the Middle Ages to lift the spirits of those who were feeling depressed and this led to them being used in exorcism rituals too.

A helpful ingredient to break negative habits and destructive cycles, it is also said to help protect a person from evil temptations…

I can't vouch for that... All these properties also make it a useful herb to bring about protection.

Grow them outside your window and/or hang bunches from the ceiling to bring protection to your house.

I also read that gypsies used to tell the fortune using chives.

Chives Magical Properties:
Exorcism, negative energy, bad habits, protection.
Ruling planet – Mars
Element – Fire
Gender – Masculine

Chocolate

(Theobroma cacao)

Now where do I start? I have to tell you I take my writing job seriously and I do a huge amount of research... This particular subject took some time... and involved a lot of practical investigation...

Chocolate is made from the cacao bean with a combination of cocoa solids, cocoa butter, fat and sugar then sometimes milk powder or condensed milk. White chocolate contains no cocoa solids, just cocoa butter, sugar and milk, which in my own opinion should be banned... Bleuch!

The darker the chocolate the higher the cocoa content. I have actually eaten 99% dark chocolate... it made my tongue stick to the roof of my mouth... not recommended, but I do like a nice 70% dark chocolate or a milk chocolate or any chocolate really – just not white...

You don't have to waste ... ahem... I mean use your actual chocolate bars in spell work; cocoa powder works very well and it doesn't melt, which is always a bonus.

We have the Mayans and the Aztecs to thank for coming up with chocolate originally in the form of a beverage, which was believed to be of divine origin (and I wholeheartedly agree).

The cacao beans were used by the Mayans for currency so

chocolate works extremely well in prosperity magic.

Chocolate makes you feel good... FACT. It raises your emotional energy and gives you a warm fuzzy feeling, so add it to any workings with that intent in mind.

Chocolate is associated with the heart chakra, so that links it perfectly with love, along with a very long tradition of presenting chocolates to a lady to win her affections.

It is also nice to take a flask of hot chocolate to rituals... to help ward off the cold when you are standing outside in the middle of a forest with the rain pouring down...

A mug of hot chocolate is also a good carrier to add other ingredients to for any magical workings.

Chocolate Magical Properties:
Prosperity, positive energy, happiness, love.
Ruling planet – Mars
Element – Fire
Gender – Feminine

Cinnamon

(Cinnamomum zeylanicum, Cinnamomum verum)
Such a fabulous scent and flavour packing a powerful punch of energy, cinnamon is made from the dried bark of the branches of the tree.

Burn cinnamon as an incense or add it to your recipes to bring focus and concentration; this will also bring about a deeper spiritual connection and boost your psychic abilities.

Add cinnamon to sachets and pouches or meals to bring about love and success. I often add a pinch of powdered cinnamon to any spell work that needs an extra boost of power. That cinnamon power punch also gives you the strength and courage to make necessary changes in your life.

Tie a bundle of cinnamon with a black or red ribbon and hang it in your hallway to bring protection, love and success to your household.

Wear a dab or two of cinnamon oil when you go on a date for added *ooh la la*. (It might be an idea to dilute it with a carrier oil first if your skin is sensitive).

Cinnamon Magical Properties:

Success, healing, power, psychic powers, protection, love, focus, lust, spirituality, changes.

Ruling planet – Sun

Element – Fire

Gender – Masculine

Clove

(Eugenia carophyllus, Syzygium aromaticum, Caryophyllus aromaticus)
One of my favourite scents and flavours, cloves are grown on a small evergreen tree. They are the beginnings of the seeds that form just after the flowers.

Add cloves to incense to clear negative energy and increase the spiritual energy in your home.

Use clove oil as a love blessing or add a couple of drops to cider, mead or wine and share with friends to bring your friendship closer. If you want to keep harmony among a group of people, charge a number of cloves with peace and friendship and then give one to each person to keep with them or bake a big apple pie studded with cloves to share with everyone. If you want to attract a lover, cloves can be carried on you for that purpose too.

Keep a clove in your purse or wallet to attract abundance. I think the idea of cloves being for prosperity came about when they were an extremely expensive spice.

Hang a pouch of cloves above your door to stop gossip and bring about protection to those within your home.

Clove Magical Properties:

Love, money, exorcism, clarity, protection, abundance, repels negativity, prevents gossip, stress relief, truth.

Ruling planet – Jupiter

Element – Fire

Gender – Masculine

Cocoa

See chocolate

Coconut

(Cocos nucifera)

The coconut tree is a member of the palm family and the nut is not actually a nut... it is a fruit called a drupe ... confused yet? It consists of three layers; the exocarp, which we don't often see in the shops or markets and which is the outermost layer, inside that is the brown coir husk (the mesocarp) that we are familiar with and contains the white coconut flesh that we know and love (or hate), and inside that is the coconut milk.

Coconuts have long been used for protection... not in the sense of hitting someone on the head with it (that might work... but not recommended), but because coconuts are hung in the home to bring protective energies in. They also work to bring purification as well.

If you happen to have two coconut shells they can be filled with protective herbs and spices then sealed together and buried on your property – kind of a coconut poppet.

Eating coconut is said to open up your spirituality.

The Greek goddess Athena is said to be partial to a drop of coconut milk, which is sacred to her.

It is a very feminine nut... or fruit... or nut... with the pure white flesh and milk contained therein.

In my research I found the property of 'chastity' mentioned alongside coconut, but never any further explanation ... until I found a practice where a whole ritual and festival surrounds the 'chastity coconut'. Once every seven years all eligible youths have dry coconuts cracked on their scalps to prove that they are either still virgins or that they have not had extra marital affairs... The more coconuts they withstand the purer they are... More than two coconuts and you are considered pure, the best score so far apparently is five.

And of course for all serious Practical Magic fans... you put the lime in the coconut...

Coconut Magical Properties:
Protection, purification, chastity.
Ruling planet – Moon
Element – Water
Gender – Feminine

Coffee
(coffea)
This is a favourite caffeine-fuelled brew made from the roasted beans (seeds) of an evergreen shrub from the *coffea* genus – usually *coffea Arabica* or *coffea canephora*.

Now I have to admit I am a bit of a coffee wuss... it has to be a latte and it has to have heap loads of caramel syrup in otherwise I don't like the taste much, but I love the smell of freshly roasted coffee.

Our wake me up, pick me up tonic has been drunk since around 800AD.

Coffee brings a magical (and practical) boost of energy and clarity of thought. Although apparently in Constantinople it was banned at one stage because it made people too clear headed...

It rates as a fire element, but I have also added water as an element too because in liquid form a higher percentage of your cup of coffee is water.

If you aren't into karma or worried about free will... coffee can be used to encourage people to come around to your way of thinking or do what you want them to. Make them a cup of coffee and add sugar to sweeten their mood, as you stir the coffee visualise your desired outcome. In hoodoo, bodily fluids are added to cups of coffee for much the same purpose...

African tribes have been known to crush the ripe coffee berries, mix them with animal fat and roll them into balls. These would then be served to those going to war providing the warriors with nourishment in the form of the fat and coffee protein and the caffeine high as a stimulant... I suspect it tasted horrible!

Coffee grounds can also be used in divination just as you would read tea leaves.

Coffee also works very well in hex-breaking or curse-breaking spells.

Add a drop of freshly brewed coffee to your bath water to help clear away illness.

Add coffee beans to your incense blends to create not only a pleasant scent, but also to bring protection to your home and dispel negative energy.

I would suggest sticking to coffee beans or freshly ground coffee for magical work rather than instant as it tends to be stronger and have better results.

Coffee Magical Properties:
Energy, clarity, divination.
Ruling planet – Mars
Element – Fire, Water
Gender – Feminine

Cookies
Cookies... are yummy... oh did you need more information than that?

They make an excellent baked item to use in ritual, especially if there are a number of people. A lot of cookie dough recipes can be shaped into crescent moons or cut out with cookie cutters into shapes to represent the ritual, spell work or sabbat that you are working with. They make excellent scrummy snacks with which to honour the deities and also to help ground you after energy work.

The cookie dough basic recipe can also be added to with spices, fruits and herbs to add in your own specific intent.

Coriander
(Coriandrum sativum)

This is an annual herb with bright green leaves growing on slim stems with pretty pale lilac flowers followed by tiny ball shaped seeds that once dried have a lovely orange scent and taste. The leaves are one of the herbs that people either love or hate the taste of.

Coriander is mentioned on Babylonian clay tablets, used by ancient Egyptians in the coffins of Emperors for protection and in the Arabian Night stories it was used as an aphrodisiac.

Use coriander to dispel negative energies and bring in protection, especially when working with astral travel.

Used for centuries as such, coriander is excellent in love potions, sachets and amulets. Hang fresh coriander leaves above your threshold to bring peace and love into your home.

Wear coriander or carry it with you to attract love and also to help release the past.

Use in health, healing and prosperity workings and recipes of all kinds.

Coriander Magical Properties:
Health, healing, peace, love, release, wealth, protection, negativity.
Ruling planet – Mars
Element – Fire
Gender – Masculine

Corn/Cornmeal

(Zea mays)

Corn is available in many guises... sweetcorn, maize, corn oil, cornmeal, corn flour/cornstarch, popcorn – the plant is tall and leafy and produces 'ears' of corn kernels.

Corn and cornmeal are good to use as offerings during the harvest sabbats and to leave as a thank you to nature. They are also good to use in spells for abundance, luck and prosperity as the corn symbolises life and abundance.

Apparently the Mayans would use the blood of their enemies to fertilise their cornfields; their king would also donate drops of his own blood (you do not want to know from which body part... really you don't...) to be sprinkled amongst the young corn plants.

The Aztecs would throw corn pollen into the air to bring rain.

Corn was and still is often used in fertility rituals and spell work.

Sigils and symbols can be drawn on the ground or on flat surfaces to invoke the gods or the spirits using cornmeal.

Corn Magical Properties:
Abundance, luck, prosperity, offerings, fertility.
Ruling planet – Sun
Element – Fire, Earth
Gender – Feminine

Crab

The shell covered sea creature is a decapod crustacean of the infra-order *Brachyura*... now you know...

Eating crab is said to help ground your spiritual energy.

The crab is sacred to the Greek god Apollo.

Because the crab looks like it is 'walking backwards', crushed crab shell can be used in magical workings to reverse hexes and curses. Don't eat it though... way too crunchy...

Crab Magical Properties:
Spirituality, hex breaking.
Ruling planet – Moon
Element – Water
Gender – Feminine

Cranberry
(Vaccinium oxycoccos)
These are creeping shrubs or vines with evergreen leaves and juicy red berries, which always make me think of Yule.

These little teeny berries of bright red goodness carry huge protective energy with them – they are a power punch against negative energy.

The cranberry doesn't seem to have a huge record of magical correspondences, not that I have found, but as it is a Mars plant then it seems to me that it would be good to use in communication workings and with its water and feminine energies it can work well in spell work for dealing with emotions.

Dried cranberries can be strung on a piece of twine or cord and made into a small wreath to hang over your doorways for protection; they also make good Yule tree decorations.

Cranberry Magical Properties:
Protection, emotions, communication.
Ruling planet – Mars
Element – Water, Fire
Gender – Feminine

Cucumber
(Cucumis sativus)
A cultivated plant from the gourd family, we must all be familiar with the cucumber... do you not have cucumber sandwiches for tea on a Sunday?

Eating the seeds of a cucumber is said to increase fertility...

However, eating slices of cucumber is said to promote chastity and curtail lustful behaviour, don't get the two confused...

Despite its obvious phallic shape, the cucumber has a very feminine energy and is ruled by the moon and the element of water, so the seeds work well in emotional spell workings.

Pop a few pieces of cucumber skin on your altar before you meditate to help with your spiritual connection.

Put out a small dish of cucumber slices in your room to soak up the negative energy and purify the room.

Eat cucumber after you have been ill, it will help the healing process.

Cucumber Magical Properties:
Fertility, emotions, chastity, meditation, spirituality, purification, healing.
Ruling planet – Moon
Element – Water
Gender – Feminine

Cumin
(Cumimum cyminum)
This has blue/green leaves and white/pink flowers in the summer followed by huge dropping seed heads, it is also very yummy in chilli and curry recipes. Cumin was once used to pay taxes with... not sure that would work now though.

Spice up any love magic workings with the fiery lust of cumin.

Sprinkle items of value with cumin to prevent them from being stolen.

Place cumin under your bed to ensure fidelity, but bear in mind that it does have a musky scent so you won't want to use a lot of it.

Wear it in an amulet to attract love and to bring about peace.

Sprinkle cumin around your property to bring in protection.

Add cumin to incense blends and recipes for abundance and success.

Cumin Magical Properties:
Exorcism, protection, anti theft, fidelity, lust, peace, love, abundance, success.
Ruling planet – Mars
Element – Fire
Gender – Masculine

Curry

Not just for a Friday night after seventeen pints of lager…

Curry powder or paste varies depending on who is making it, but often it starts with the base mix of ginger, turmeric and cumin with other spices added into it – coriander, cardamom etc.

You could make your own magical curry powder blend to incorporate different properties from each spice you add.

Curries bring with them the fire of passion and a huge boost of energy.

Curry Magical Properties:
Energy, passion.
Ruling planet – Mars
Element – Fire
Gender – Masculine

Curry Leaves

(Murraya Koenigii)
The sweet neem leaf or curry leaves come from the Murraya Koenigii plant and are used in South Indian cooking.

Burn dried curry leaves neat or in incense blends and add to recipes to provide protection.

Curry Leaves Magical Properties:
Protection.
Ruling planet – Mars
Element – Fire
Gender – Masculine

Dates

(Phoenix dactylifera)

Those suspicious looking brown wrinkled things you get at Yule (no, not grandma…). Dates are sweet fruits from the phoenix palm tree.

They are an ancient fruit… not the packet of dates from last Yule, but the tree and us eating them. They were sacred in Babylon and ancient Greece and quite often used as offerings to the gods.

The Persians used them to celebrate with the symbolism of death and resurrection.

The dried date fruit is considered to be very spiritual and symbolises the soul, they also have very strong aphrodisiac qualities… or so I am told…

They are also the ingredient in sticky toffee pudding that makes the pudding sticky.

Dates Magical Properties:
Spirituality, death and rebirth, offerings.
Ruling planet – Sun
Element – Air
Gender – Feminine

Eggs

From teeny tiny quails eggs up to huge ostrich eggs, they come in all sorts of shapes, the delicate outer casing containing the yolk and the white. Boiled, scrambled, fried, poached or sunny side up… how do you like yours?

An egg is a complete neat package of life and is very symbolic of fertility, new life, new beginnings and creation itself. Within they also symbolise long life and immortality.

Eggs were considered sacred in many cultures for centuries and a hardboiled egg was seen as magic in the Middle Ages.

Very symbolic at Ostara the egg, more often in its chocolate form, has become a part of spring celebrations as a representation of new life and new beginnings.

In legend faeries would consume eggs of mythical birds such as the phoenix.

Throughout history people have eaten eggs for lots of different reasons, some to absorb the magical properties by eating them, others to ensure fertility.

In the Slavonic and Germanic lands people also smeared eggs onto their hoes to ensure fertility for the soil.

In Iran brides and grooms exchange eggs for fertility.

In 17th century France, a bride would break an egg when she entered her new home for the first time.

Eggs were often used for divination. This stemmed from the belief that eggs symbolised life and particularly life in the future. One method involved painting the eggs, boiling them and reading the patterns in their cracks. Another method involved tossing the eggs and divining the future, a system of divination known as oomancy. Egg white can also be used, by dripping it into a bowl of water and reading the shapes that it makes.

In Egypt eggs were hung in the temples to bring fertility, for birth and renewal.

The Hindu description of the beginning of the world saw it as a cosmic egg.

The yolk in the centre of the egg has also been used to represent the sun.

I have put the gender as both masculine and feminine. In Chinese culture the egg as a flavour is seen as yang, which is masculine, but I see the egg as very feminine because of it being literally a baby chick.

The egg is a complete set of elements in one handy pack: the shell represents earth, the inner membrane represents air, the yolk is fire and the white is water.

Eggs Magical Properties:
Fertility, creation, life, new beginnings, divination.

Element – Water, Earth, Air, Fire
Gender – Masculine/Feminine

Egg Shells

Cascarilla is made from egg shells that have been crushed and ground to a powder. It is used in hoodoo and folk magic as well as other magical practices. The powder can be dusted on the body to protect from spirit possession and also acts as a shield from psychic or magical attack. It can be sprinkled around the perimeter of your home to create a peaceful environment and to protect from intruders. It can also be used for drawing runes, sigils or other symbols in rituals and workings.

Egg Shell Magical Properties:
Protection, peace.
Element – Earth
Gender – Masculine

Endive

(Cichorium endivia/crispum)
Endive is a leafy vegetable belonging to the chicory genus; it can be cooked or eaten raw.

Eating the leaves supposedly brings on lustful thoughts… as you are eating a salad leaf the lustful thoughts may well be about cake…

Carry the leaves with you to attract love, but the power of the leaves doesn't last long so you will need to replace them every three days.

Endive Magical Properties:
Lust, love.
Ruling planet – Jupiter
Element – Air, Fire
Gender – Masculine

Fennel

(Foeniculum vulgare)

Here we are dealing with Florence fennel that produces the white bulb that is eaten as a vegetable with a slight aniseed flavour (rather than the fennel seeds, although they have similar magical properties). The fennel bulb makes both a lovely salad vegetable or a cooked one.

Fennel is sacred to the Greek god Dionysus and was used in a lot of festivals and ceremonies.

Because of its aniseed flavour, fennel is very good for purification and also for personal protection. Its refreshing taste also brings healing energies too.

Fennel Magical Properties:
Purification, protection, healing.
Ruling planet – Mercury
Element – Fire
Gender – Masculine

Figs

(Ficus carica)

The fruit of the fig is borne from a deciduous tree that has scented leaves; the fruit can be used fresh or dried.

The small and perfectly formed fig is a very ancient fruit; Egyptian priests would eat a fig at the end of consecration ceremonies. In ancient Greece the fig was a sacred fruit and could not be picked until the local priest had decided they were ready.

The fig symbolises the rewards of meditation practice.

Keep fresh figs in your home to bring luck and abundance. This also works if you have one of the *Ficus* family of plants.

Offer someone a fig and allow them to eat it while you are holding the fruit. This apparently makes them fall for you...

Carve a phallic image from fig wood and carry with you to

ensure fertility. Eating fresh figs will bring about the same fertile energies.

Using a fresh fig leaf, write a question that you would like an answer to on it. If the leaf dries slowly then the answer is yes; if it dries quickly the answer is no.

I have stated both masculine and feminine energies for the fig because the flower from the plant is unisexual.

Figs Magical Properties:
Meditation, love, fertility, divination.
Ruling planet – Jupiter
Element – Air, Fire
Gender – Masculine/Feminine

Fish

This is a huge food group that covers everything from fish fingers and tuna to Dover sole and trout.

The fish is often associated with fertility, abundance and prosperity.

I tend to associate fish with the magical properties of the element of water so that covers emotions, healing, cleansing and purification as well.

Fish Magical Properties:
Fertility, prosperity, abundance, healing, emotions, cleansing, purification.
Element – Water
Gender – Feminine

Flour

Flour makes cakes... and bread... and yummy stuff.

There are many different types of flour and each will take on the energies from the grain that it was milled from.

Flour Magical Properties:
Various depending on the type of grain.
Element – Earth

Game

Game is classified as any animal hunted for food or not normally domesticated. To me that covers things like venison, pheasant, wild boar, partridge etc.

The Egyptians believed that the soul of a pharaoh ascended to the heavens in the form of a goose and geese were sacrificed at the winter solstice in many cultures to ensure that the summer returned.

In Chinese culture eating fowl ensures fidelity and faithfulness.

As a lot of wild birds migrate they were considered a big part of the cycle of nature (as all animals are actually), but divination was used following their migration patterns.

Eating the meat from game was believed to imbue the attributes and characteristics of the animal to the person eating them, such as speed, intelligence, courage and power.

Game covers all the elements depending on the animal, duck would be water and air, pheasant would be air and earth, boar would be earth and fire etc.

Game Magical Properties:
Fidelity, divination, power, energy.
Element – Fire, Air, Earth, Water
Gender – Masculine

Garlic

(Allium sativum)
I will not make any vampire jokes... I will not make any vampire jokes...

Garlic is incredibly beneficial to your health (still not making any vampire jokes...) and brilliant to use in magical workings.

Garlic is sacred to the Greek goddess Hecate and can be left at a crossroads as an offering to her.

Carry garlic with you to provide personal protection and hang bulbs of garlic in your home to protect against thieves and evil spirits (not mentioning vampires…). Carrying garlic with you should also provide protection against psychic attacks.

It is a brilliant ingredient to use in any protection or hex breaking workings and wonderful to dispel negative energies… and vampires (doh… failed…)

Eat garlic to induce lust… but maybe not too much because garlic breath will definitely outweigh the lust effects.

Garlic salt is a useful ingredient to use in magical workings as it carries the properties of garlic and salt and it is in a manageable format to add to pouches and witches' bottles. You can also use the white papery skin of the garlic bulb in magical workings; it has the same properties but smells less pungent.

Images of garlic have been found in Egyptian tombs depicted as offerings to the gods and apparently those who built the pyramids were paid partly in garlic.

Roman soldiers ate garlic before going into battle to give them strength and courage.

Burn garlic skins in your house to keep money coming in, to help dispel negative energy and ease depression.

Remove illness by rubbing a fresh clove of garlic over the body where the problem lies then throw the garlic bulb away into running water or bury it at a crossroads.

Hanging a braid of garlic in your home should discourage unpleasant visitors.

Garlic Magical Properties:
Healing, protection, hex breaking, negative energies, lust, strength, courage, depression.
Ruling planet – Mars

Element – Fire
Gender – Masculine

Ginger
(Zingiber officinale)
Ginger is the rhizome from the *Zingiber officinale* plant. The root can be used fresh (peel it first) or dried and used as powder.

Sliced root ginger dropped into hot water with a splash of honey and a sprinkling of cinnamon makes a delicious drink.

In some parts of the world it was traditional to chew raw ginger then spit it onto a diseased area of the body to cure the illness. Don't they know it's rude to spit?

Ginger does have huge healing properties, not just medicinally but also magically, so add it to healing pouches, witches' bottles and incense blends.

Ginger also packs a spicy punch, so add it to magical workings to boost the energy. It can also be used to speed things up and bring about a successful outcome. Eat some ginger before your spell work to increase your magical power. In fact you can add it to any recipe to boost the magical intent.

Ginger has a history of being used in love and passion spells so for that romantic meal spice it up with a hit of ginger.

Make a simple ginger oil by infusing root ginger into base oil and then anoint your purse or wallet with the oil to keep money coming in.

Folklore says that growing a ginger plant from the root placed in water in your home will attract good health and prosperity.

Hang a piece of root ginger over your doorway to bring protection to your house and sprinkle powdered ginger around your property to keep trouble out.

Ginger Magical Properties:
Healing, power, love, passion, success, prosperity, protection.
Ruling planet – Mars

Element – Fire
Gender – Masculine

Grapefruit
(Citrus paradise)
The grapefruit is a hybrid citrus fruit from a liaison between the pomelo and the sweet orange. It was very popular in the 1970s to have for breakfast, but it seems to have fallen a little out of fashion.

Grapefruit is a sharp refreshing taste and scent so can be used to bring about happiness and lift your spirits and your mood. It also awakens the body, mind and soul and helps open you up to the spirit world. It also gives a good energy boost.

Grapefruit is a good purifying fruit and often used in detoxes.

Grapefruit Magical Properties:
Happiness, spirit work, purification, depression, energy.
Ruling planet – Jupiter, Sun
Element – Fire, Water
Gender – Feminine

Grapes
(Vitis vinifera)
Grapes are the clusters of berries from a deciduous woody vine. They can be eaten in all sorts of ways including fresh just as they are or made into jam, juice, jelly, vinegar, oil, dried to make raisins or what I am sure is the most preferred way to ingest them... wine.

Don't just think about using the fruit of the grape in your recipes, remember the vine leaves too.

Grapes have a huge spiritual energy to them and can help us with spiritual connection, visions and dreams.

Whenever I think about Greek or Roman temples I visualise them surrounded by grape vines.

Eating grapes is said to increase your fertility... although too much grape in its wine format may not help in this particular area...

The grape is a moon-ruled fruit so works very well in all kinds of moon magic.

The grape is also symbolic of abundance and the harvest and associated with the Egyptian goddess Hathor, the Roman god Bacchus and the Greek god Dionysus.

To make a simple prosperity talisman wrap a vine leaf around a shiny silver coin and tie it with green or orange string or ribbon; carry it with you to bring prosperity your way.

Planting grapevines on your property helps to bring abundance into your home.

Use wine to asperge the earth before you cast a circle or as an offering to deity... actually pouring wine onto the ground has to be a sacrificial and giving act in itself!

Grapes Magical Properties:
Spiritual, fertility, moon magic.
Ruling planet – Moon
Element – Air, Water
Gender – Feminine

Gravy

Yep even gravy has magical properties... aside from being absolutely scrummy of course... but no lumps please.

Gravy pours ... so it aids in the smooth transition of projects, plans and situations. It also carries with it the magical properties of water – emotions, healing, cleansing and purification.

Gravy can also sooth the sometimes aggressive quality of meat in your recipes.

Gravy Magical Properties:
Calming, emotions, healing, cleansing, purification.
Ruling planet – Moon

Element – Water
Gender – Feminine

Guava
(Psidium guajava)
This is a tropical fruit that grows on a small tree from the myrtle family... I just love the name Myrtle... it makes me think of a batty little old lady who lives with 27 cats...

The guava is a fruit of the romantic fairy tale bringing romance, love and an air of seeing the world through rose coloured glasses... let's just hope it has a happy ending...

The guava is also a good fruit for purification and cleansing.

Guava Magical Properties:
Love, romance, purification.
Ruling planet – Venus
Element – Water
Gender – Feminine

Hazelnut
(Corylus)
Hazelnut is the nut from the hazel tree (no big surprise there) sometimes known as cobnut.

Whilst writing about the hazelnut all I had in my head was:

What has a hazelnut in every bite?
...squirrel droppings...

Yep I know... I should lay off the coffee before writing...

The hazelnut is sacred to the god Thor and hazel twigs can be placed around the home to protect your house from being struck by lightning.

Eating hazelnuts stimulates the third eye chakra and enhances your psychic powers and intuition.

The little hazelnut is also packed full of the magical properties of wisdom and fertility, snack on a few hazelnuts if your brain is in a fog, it should provide clarity.

String hazelnuts onto a cord and hang in your home to bring in the magic of the faerie world.

The hazelnut also has a huge amount of medicinal healing properties.

I associate the hazelnut with both male and female energies because the flowers are both – the catkins are male, but the tree also produces tiny female flowers that hide in the leaves.

The nuts can also be ground into flour for making bread or cakes.

In the legend of Finn MacCaul (Fionn MacCumhail) hazelnuts fell around a sacred pool that was surrounded by nine hazel trees. The salmon that lived in the water ate the hazelnuts and was filled with infinite knowledge... then Finn ate the salmon and the knowledge was passed to him. Although this does beg the question... if the salmon was filled with infinite knowledge, why did he allow someone to catch and eat him?

Hazelnut Magical Properties:
Protection, psychic powers, wisdom, fertility, faerie, healing.
Ruling planet – Sun, Mercury
Element – Air
Gender – Feminine/Masculine

Honey

Honey – the glorious nectar of the bees. It is one of the oldest foods known to man... and woman. Bees are incredibly magical and are often said to be messengers from the gods and the spirit world.

Honey is sacred to many gods including the Egyptian god Ra and the Greek goddesses Artemis and Demeter and the Hindu gods Vishnu and Krishna.

It is incredibly beneficial medicinally, but also brings a good dollop of happiness with it.

Honey can be added to any spell work or any culinary recipe to sweeten someone's mood or disposition.

Honey makes an excellent offering to the gods, the spirits and the faerie world.

Add a drop of honey to incense blends to sweeten the mood.

Honey works well for happiness, love, prosperity and healing. It can also add a bit of zing to your love life too.

Tell it to the bees... they are great listeners... when a beekeeper dies, folklore says that the survivors must tell the bees of their keeper's death and persuade them to stay rather than follow their keeper to the otherworld.

Anything important should be told to the bees, such as marriages, births and other important events, but make sure you whisper politely.

Bees are also considered to be an image of the human soul, perhaps due to their natural ability to find their way home from great distances... If my soul were in a bee it would still get lost!

And more importantly... honey is used to make mead, which is absolutely delicious and wonderful to use in ritual and offerings... Half a glass and I am away with the faeries... who actually like a drop of mead or honey as well...

In the Terry Pratchett Discworld stories the main witch, Granny Weatherwax, gets her news from the bees, the see all and know all (if you haven't read any Discworld stories... then why not?... Go and read one now!)

Honey Magical Properties:
Happiness, healing, love, prosperity, passion, spirituality, faerie.
Element – Water, Earth
Gender – Feminine

Horseradish
(Armoracia rusticana)
Horseradish is the root of a perennial plant cultivated for

culinary use, but can often be found growing in the wild too. The flavour has a huge powerful hot kick to it.

Legend tells us that the Delphic oracle told Apollo, 'The radish is worth its weight in lead, the beet its weight in silver, the horseradish its weight in gold.'

The horseradish brings a very strong masculine energy that vitalises and purifies not just the body, but the soul too.

Sprinkle dried horseradish root around the boundaries of your home to provide protection.

Ancient Greeks ate horseradish as an aphrodisiac.

Horseradish Magical Properties:
Protection, energy, purification, passion.
Ruling planet – Mars
Element – Fire
Gender – Masculine

Ice Cream

Real ice cream, not the frozen yogurt stuff. Although quite a lot of the products sold in the supermarket under the guise of 'ice cream' these days don't even have any cream in them, just lots of fats instead. Proper full fat cream ice cream is totally indulgent and incredibly lush. It brings with it the magic of the moon and huge amounts of feminine energies… grab a spoon…

You can of course add all sorts of different magical energies to ice cream just by adding flavours to it, so vanilla ice cream for instance would bring the energy of love with it and mint choc chip ice cream would bring healing, purification, money and love – all rolled up into one scrummy spoonful.

You can make/get savoury ice creams. I have tasted avocado ice cream and tomato… weird is an understatement…

The milk that ice cream is made from brings the magical properties of love and spirituality.

Ice Cream Magical Properties:
Love, spirituality, various depending on what flavours you add.
Ruling planet – Moon
Element – Water
Gender – Feminine

Jelly

Now what goes well with ice cream? Jelly of course! This is another 'base' recipe that you can add all kinds of flavours to and therefore all kinds of magical properties. Jelly also makes me think of my childhood, so I believe that it also brings happiness and childlike joy with it.

Jelly Magical Properties:
Happiness, various – depending on what flavours you add.

Juice

Juice is an incredibly versatile ingredient that can be made from fruits or vegetables, each one with a different magical property.

Juice Magical Properties:
Various – depending on what fruit or vegetable you use.

Kiwifruit

(Actinidia deliciosa)

This is a funny little fruit covered in fuzzy hair, but inside it has the most beautiful bright green flesh with black seeds and a white centre. (Sometimes called a Chinese gooseberry). Apparently the fruit was named after the New Zealand kiwi bird.

My research turned up this little nugget of information – the kiwifruit is considered by some cultures to be plant testicles... and eaten to encourage passion and romance. I may never be able to look at a kiwifruit in the same light again...

Kiwifruit Magical Properties:
Love, romance.
Ruling planet – Moon
Element – Water, Earth
Gender – Masculine

Kumquat

(Rutaceae Fortunella)

This has to be one of the best names for a fruit doesn't it?

The fruits are also called kinkan and are produced from small evergreen trees that have pretty white blossoms in the summer.

They are a beautiful golden yellow/orange colour and add a bright touch of sunshiny magic to any dish, use them to bring in the magical energy that the sun brings with it. The kumquat is also considered to be a lucky fruit that brings money with it too.

Kumquat Magical Properties:
Sun energy, luck, money.
Ruling planet – Sun
Element – Air
Gender – Masculine

Lamb

Lamb is basically a baby sheep – young, fluffy and bouncing around the fields, so think of all the properties that spring (pun intended) to mind when you see that image... sensitivity, caring, nurturing, the season of spring, new life and new beginnings.

Throughout history the lamb has also been used – sometimes just symbolically – as a sacrifice for the life force that it carries.

Sheep have also been revered for centuries with many civilisations having dedicated gods and goddesses that were prayed to for protection over their flocks of sheep. The sheep were an important part of life, not only providing food, but also producing clothing. In fact a few of the gods have been depicted wearing rams' horns on their heads.

Lamb Magical Properties:
Caring, nurture, new life, beginnings, spring, fertility.
Element – Fire, Earth
Gender – Masculine

Leeks
(Allium ampeloprasum)
Part of the *allium* family along with garlic and onions the leek carries a lot of similar magical energies. Use it to drive away evil, bring protection and release impurities.

The leek is also associated with all kinds of love magic.

Plant leeks around your house to bring in protection.

Historically leeks were carried into battle to provide protection; personally I think a shield would have been better...

The leek, along with the onion, is sacred to the Norse god Thor.

Leeks Magical Properties:
Purification, protection, love.
Ruling planet – Mars
Element – Fire
Gender – Masculine

Lemon
(Citrus x lemon)
These little bright yellow fruits are sacred to the moon and bring with them her beautiful powers, but I also think that the colour of the fruit brings the happiness of the sun's energy too.

The acidic taste of lemon juice means it works very well magically for purification, but the scent is also very uplifting and is said to help with decision-making.

Lemon juice works well as an asperge or in a ritual bath. The leaves of a lemon tree or dried lemon peel can be added to incense blends, bath water, spiritual washes or medicine bags.

The flowers of the lemon tree and lemon rind work well in love magic.

Lemon pie apparently brings with it fidelity and offering a slice of lemon to a stranger will guarantee their friendship.

Lemon can also be used to provide protection – whether you make up a witches' bottle containing lemon peel or just throw the fruit at an intruder… because if you hit them it would certainly sting…

You could also stick a lemon with coloured pins and hang it in the house to bring blessings. Or stick nine iron nails into a lemon and tie it with red thread then hang it beside your front door to ward away evil.

Lemon Magical Properties:
Purification, moon magic, happiness, decisions, uplifting, love, protection, friendship, fidelity.
Ruling planet – Moon
Element – Water
Gender – Feminine

Lemongrass
(Cymbopogon citrates)
Lemongrass is a tall perennial grass used a lot in Asian cooking and herbal teas. It has a mild citrus taste and can be used fresh, dried or powdered.

Use lemongrass to bring out your happy playful side, which also works well in connecting with the world of faerie.

Lemongrass as an essential oil also works well for divination and ceremonial magic uses and is said to help aid you in taking on board magical knowledge.

Lemongrass also brings with it the magical properties of shape shifting.

Lemongrass Magical Properties:
Faerie magic, happiness, divination, ceremonial, knowledge, shape shifting.
Ruling planet – Mercury
Element – Fire
Gender – Masculine

Lettuce

(Lactuca sativa)
It is that green leafy stuff that they tell you is healthy, but actually tastes of soggy paper... can you tell I think lettuce is a waste of space?

Anyway... it does have some special magical properties.

Use lettuce for fertility and to honour the Egyptian god Min. It can also be added to love magic workings.

Apparently, so the story goes... the local variety of lettuce in ancient Egypt was phallic shaped and when cut or torn the stems released a milky juice... hence the connection to the fertility god Min... I am not saying a word...

Eat lettuce to help with meditation and to create a calm and centred mind for astral travel.

Lettuce Magical Properties:
Fertility, meditation, astral travel, calm.
Ruling planet – Moon
Element – Water
Gender – Neutral

Lime

(Citrus aurantifolia)
The green version of a lemon, OK I know it's more complicated than that... the lime generally has a more sour taste to it than lemon.

Just like the lemon though, the lime is good for purification and cleansing. And whereas the lemon is a moon fruit the lime balances that out by being a fruit ruled by the sun.

In Malaysia the magic makers use limes for love spells, to release disease, to provide protection against evil and to protect pregnant mothers and newborn babies.

Evil spirits are said to absolutely hate limes, which makes it perfect for cleansing rituals and purifying your home.

Limes are also good for bringing a good boost of energy.

Lime Magical Properties:
Purification, love, healing, protection, energy.
Ruling planet –Sun
Element – Fire
Gender – Masculine

Liquorice
(Glycyrrhiza glabra)
The liquorice plant is of the legume family and the sweet liquorice taste is extracted from the root of the plant. It is very much a 'love or hate' kind of taste.

It is said… those who eat liquorice will become more potent lovers…

Liquorice not only brings the magical property of fertility with it (see note above re potent lovers), but it also brings balance.

I have eaten liquorice flavour ice cream and it was divine.

Liquorice Magical Properties:
Love, passion, balance.
Ruling planet – Venus, Mercury
Element – Earth, Water
Gender – Feminine

Liver
Liver – and in fact any offal from an animal – will carry the magical energies of that specific animal with it. Liver also carries

courage and power; some ancient tribes would eat the livers of their enemies to assimilate their strength. Definitely a warrior energy!

Romans would use the offal of sacrificed animals to predict the future, but I am not sure that would go down particularly well these days at your dinner party...

Liver Magical Properties:
Courage, power.
Element – Fire

Lobster

A very imposing looking sea crustacean, the lobster is not as cartoons would have you believe red in colour... until it has been cooked... so yes, all those Disney lobster characters have actually been boiled...

Lobster carries the magical energies of the sea, as most sea creatures do, but the lobster is also sacred to Ares, the Greek god of war.

Lobster Magical Properties:
Sea magic, power, courage.
Element – Water, Fire
Gender – Masculine

Macadamia

(Macadamia spp)

A nut from trees indigenous to Australia, the macadamia is a nut of luxury; it is big and rich tasting so it stands to reason that this nut works well magically for prosperity and abundance.

Macadamia Magical Properties:
Prosperity.
Ruling planet – Jupiter

Element – Earth
Gender – Masculine

Mango
(Mangifera indica)
This is a juicy tropical fruit that tastes delicious once you have wrestled the fruit away from the huge stone that resides inside…

The mango is sacred to Buddha and carries with it a very strong spiritual energy. Buddha was given a mango grove as a gift and would spend hours sitting under the trees in meditation.

The mango was first mentioned in Sanskrit written documents in India more than 6,000 years ago.

The wood from a mango tree is used in India to prepare pyres for the dead and lovers are said to express their feelings under the branches of the mango tree. Mango leaves are used in marriage ceremonies to represent love and fertility. Mango branches were put above doorways of a house where a new birth had occurred.

It is said that to eat the fruit of the mango can promote sexual excitement… you have been warned.

Mango Magical Properties:
Spirituality, love, fertility, passion.
Ruling planet – Mars
Element – Fire, Air
Gender – Feminine

Maple Syrup
This lush sticky syrup is made from the xylem sap of the maple tree and is a definite must have on any stack of pancakes.

Maple syrup is associated with long life and abundance. The leaves of maple are used in love and money rituals and spell work.

Basically the syrup carries all the magical properties of the maple tree… but in an edible format.

The maple tree is one of attraction, drawing in and bringing things together, and is generally a very happy and positive tree. It also works well in bindings because of its stickiness...

Maple wands are often used for spiritual healing so I see no reason why maple syrup can't be used for the same intent.

Maple Syrup Magical Properties:
Love, money, attraction, positive energy, healing, binding.
Ruling planet – Jupiter
Element – Earth, Water
Gender – Masculine and Feminine

Margarine

I am not a huge fan of margarine because, let's face it, with the amount of chemicals and unidentifiable ingredients that go into making margarine it is never going to taste like butter... but it does spread straight from the fridge.

It will carry the magical properties of whatever vegetable oil it was made from and some even contain real milk *shock* so it will also have those energies too.

Margarine Magical Properties:
Various – depending on the vegetable oil used.
Element – Water

Marjoram
(Origanum majorana)
I grow several varieties of marjoram in my garden, but it also grows in the wild on dry grassland and waste ground. The plant is a perennial growing up to 2 feet high with slender stems and small oval leaves. Lilac coloured flowers appear in the summer. It is often referred to as sweet or knotted marjoram.

Greeks and Romans wove garlands of marjoram for betrothed couples to wear, making it an excellent herb to use in love workings and marriage spells. Put a bundle of marjoram under your pillow to dream of your future love.

It is a happy herb and can be used in happiness and anti-depression spell work and recipes as well as very successfully for aiding with grief.

Sprinkle marjoram leaves around your house for protection. Hang a bunch over your threshold for the same purpose.

Add a sprinkle of marjoram to your bathwater to help you stay healthy and to keep bugs at bay.

It is also very nice in pasta sauce.

Marjoram Magical Properties:
Love, happiness, health, protection, marriage, grief.
Ruling planet – Mercury
Element – Air
Gender – Masculine

Melon
This is the fleshy round/oval fruit from the Cucurbitaceae family that comes in all sorts of varieties.

You can eat melon to take on the magical properties, but the seeds also work well in medicine pouches, witches' bottles and incense blends.

Apparently during the Middle Ages melons were regarded with great suspicion, eating one would make you more vulnerable to the plague… or so they said…

Watermelon is one of the oldest varieties of melon and is sacred to the Egyptian god of disorder, Set. So there you go… melons represent chaos, who knew?

The melon does have that look and feel of 'health' about it so it does work well for healing and cleansing magic and it also works well for the magical energy of 'the lurve thang'… note I have not mentioned anything at all about melons representing lady bumps…

Melon Magical Properties:
Love, chaos, healing, purification.
Ruling planet – Moon
Element – Water
Gender – Feminine

Milk

Milk… comes from cows, sheep, goats and yaks… possibly some other animals, but not ones that I can purchase milk from in my local shops (although to be fair they don't sell yak milk either).

It used to be that the milkman delivered bottles of milk to your doorstep and you got full fat and nothing else, now you can get milk in all sorts of guises from full fat deliciousness to completely skimmed, which looks and tastes like water. When I lived on a farm we used to go to the dairy and scoop out a jug of still warm milk from the tank where the cows had just been milked. It was thick and luscious and delicious, although now that would be totally against all sorts of health and safety stupidity rules.

Milk is produced by the mother to feed the infant so it carries with it beautiful nurturing energies, heap loads of feminine power and amazing goddess energy too. It is also ruled by the moon so you get her energy in there as well.

Brilliant for using as offerings and libations during ritual and when you are out and want to leave an offering on the ground or for a tree spirit, the faeries are partial to a drop of milk too especially if you add in a drop of honey.

Pour a libation of milk into the sea to honour the goddess Isis. Milk is also sacred to Hathor and Zeus.

I believe milk also carries with it the magical properties of the animal it came from.

Milk Magical Properties:
Feminine power, goddess energy, moon magic, nurturing, offerings, love, spirituality, faeries.

Ruling planet – Moon
Element – Water
Gender – Feminine

Mint

(Mentha spp, Mentha aquatic, Mentha piperita)
This aromatic perennial with dense lilac flowers is usually grown in gardens, but can be found in the wild beside streams and in damp woodlands. There are a huge amount of varieties.

I have it in my garden, but keep it restricted in a pot otherwise it would take over the world, you have been warned.

Use peppermint oil on your forehead and the corners of your books (yeah I know, I can't bring myself to put it on my books either) to aid concentration.

Drinking mint tea can help with keeping communications sweet.

The scent is uplifting and positive and can also be used in travel spells.

Mint can be cooling, so I think it works well in spell work and recipes to 'cool down' a situation.

Add a few sprigs of fresh mint to a glass of water to cleanse and purify your body from the inside out.

Add mint to your floor wash to clear and cleanse the home.

Place peppermint leaves under your pillow for a calm and restful sleep.

Keep a mint leaf in your purse or wallet to ensure money keeps coming in.

Peppermint has lots of cooling and calming medicinal properties so use it in healing spells too.

Sprinkle mint around your property to provide protection from negative energy.

Mint Magical Properties:
Money, healing, exorcism, protection, cleansing, calming.

Ruling planet – Mercury, Venus
Element – Air
Gender – Masculine

Mushrooms

We shall focus here on the edible fungi variety as opposed to the hallucinogenic mushrooms...

You can forage for many types of mushroom in the wild, but please make sure you have identified them correctly as there are a lot of poisonous varieties that could make you very sick... or worse...

Mushrooms can be eaten to gain strength and courage; I think this stems from the belief that the mushroom is a vegetable substitute for 'flesh' given its texture.

The fact that quite often mushrooms seem to appear magically overnight and that they appear frequently as a faerie ring entitles them to a bit of magic and mysticism.

They are an interesting food as they bring both the feminine energies of the moon, but also the grounding energy of the earth bringing about a good balance.

Mushrooms Magical Properties:
Strength, courage, magic, balance.
Ruling planet – Moon
Element – Earth
Gender – Feminine

Mustard

(Brassica juncea, Brassica nigra, Sinapis hirta)
Mustard the condiment is made from the seeds of a mustard plant, which are ground or cracked and mixed with water, salt and usually lemon juice (other liquid is sometimes used).

For magical or edible purposes you can use the seeds or the condiment.

The mustard seed appears in many ancient texts and stories including the Bible, Jewish texts and stories about Buddha quite often refer to the mustard seed as representing faith or the universe.

Mustard is sacred to the Greek god of healing Aesclepius and was/is used to treat a huge array of ailments.

Mustard increases alertness and opens up your higher mental and psychic channels bringing clarity and insight.

Sprinkle mustard seeds around your property to bring in protection.

Eat mustard seeds to assist with astral travel. Hindus believe that eating mustard seeds allows them to have out-of-body experiences to enable them to gain insight into the universe.

Carry a medicine pouch filled with mustard seeds to bring protection, faith and success. Black mustard seeds are for protection and white mustard seeds are for faith and success.

Sprinkle black mustard seeds and sulphur powder onto an enemy's garden to cause disruption and trouble (watch out for karma, or the concept of three-fold return, though...).

Black mustard seeds can also be used in workings to disrupt the actions of people who are causing you grief or harm.

Mustard Magical Properties:
Clarity, psychic abilities, protection, astral travel, faith, success.
Ruling planet – Mars
Element – Fire
Gender – Masculine

Nectarine
(Prunus spp)
Basically a nectarine is a bald peach... completely fluffless.

The name derives from the Greek *nectar*, the food of the gods.

The nectarine is ruled by Venus and the element of water and is a total love fruit.

Nectarine Magical Properties:
Love.
Ruling planet – Venus
Element – Water
Gender – Feminine

Nutmeg
(Myristica fragrans)
Nutmeg hails from a tall tree with smooth greyish bark that flowers three times a year. It takes nine years before the tree produces its first crop. The nutmeg we are familiar with is the seed, which is covered by an outer shell that we know as mace. They are separated and then dried.

Carry nutmeg with you for good luck and to attract money to you. A whole nutmeg makes an excellent good luck charm.

Sprinkle nutmeg (powdered not lots of whole ones…) around your property to protect against negative energy.

Keep a whole nutmeg under your bed to ensure that fidelity in your relationship stays solid.

Nutmeg is sometimes used in place of High John the Conqueror in spell work.

Nutmeg Magical Properties:
Money, luck, fidelity, protection.
Ruling planet – Jupiter
Element – Fire
Gender – Masculine

Oats
(Avena sativa)
This cereal grain is grown for its seed, which produces the oats and oatmeal we are familiar with for our breakfast … Oh and in flapjacks… don't forget flapjacks… and oatmeal cookies…

The grain is big on fertility and that sexual vibe baby…

There was a belief (centuries ago) that oats caused mental and physical disorders. Thankfully after being cultivated in around 100AD the humble oat became a symbol of prosperity, so eat it to bring the money in or add to your spell work.

During the Middle Ages the oat was believed to attract vampires, so farmers added garlic bulbs to their property. Quite what a vampire would want from a bowl of porridge I don't know...

Oats Magical Properties:
Passion, fertility, prosperity.
Ruling planet – Venus
Element – Earth
Gender – Feminine

Oils

The magical properties of the oil you use will depend on the vegetable from which it originated.

Oil is very versatile being used in cooking, burnt in lamps, added to ointments and salves, as essential oil for a variety of uses and as lubrication.

You can add to your basic oils and flavour them with chillies, black pepper, garlic and all kinds of herbs, not only to add to the taste, but also to bring in other magical properties.

Oils Magical Properties:
Various – depending on the type of vegetable.
Element – Water

Olives

(Olea europaea)
The fruit of the olive tree comes in hundreds of varieties and colours, and of course is the source of olive oil.

I wish I liked olives, they look very opulent and regal, but for me they taste like a mouthful of perfume... yuck!

However, they are also a very spiritual fruit and represent your spiritual goals as well as integrity.

The olive is sacred to the Egyptian solar god Aten.

The cross of Jesus was also apparently made from olive wood.

Eat olives to help with your *va va voom* and to increase fertility.

Olive oil is also good for anointing and using as a base for anointing oil blends and is excellent in healing spell work.

The olive branch has long been a symbol of peace, so share a bowl of olives to bring about peace after an argument.

Hang olive branches or leaves in your home to bring about protection and carry olive leaves with you for luck.

Olives Magical Properties:
Spirituality, integrity, passion, fertility, healing, peace, protection, luck.
Ruling planet – Sun
Element – Fire, Air
Gender – Masculine

Onions
(Allium cepa)
The good ol' onion has to be one of the most commonly used vegetables in cooking.

Onions and garlic were apparently fed to the labourers who built the Great Pyramid of Khufu and some ancient Egyptians paid their workers with onions.

The Egyptians also believed that onions absorbed negative energy and impurities and also used onions to swear oaths upon.

Onions have historically been used to protect against infectious diseases and often used in exorcism.

The humble onion is good for sexual energy and fertility, but I would not recommend eating it raw before any kind of romantic encounter... you don't want to be giving onion flavoured snogs… just saying…

Eat onions for physical and spiritual health and protection.

Onion Magical Properties:
Passion, fertility.
Ruling planet – Mars
Element – Fire
Gender – Masculine

Orange

(Citrus × sinensis)
The orange coloured citrus fruit, you know the one.

The orange is a fruit of the sun, a fruit of love and happiness and a fruit with an enlightening and uplifting scent.

During the 19th century to give a gift of an orange was thought to be generous and thoughtful. (Just for the record I prefer gifts of chocolate).

Orange is good for purifying the mind, body and spirit. Orange juice makes a good ritual drink and orange peel makes a good herbal tea to help bring about clarity and energy.

Dried orange peel also works well in incense blends to represent the energy of the sun, but doesn't smell particularly good when burnt. Try dropping a few orange peels into an oil burner with a base oil to release the scent.

Oranges are sacred to the god of earth and air, Enlil.

Orange water can be used to flavour dishes especially if you are entertaining a loved one. Bathe in orange water to attract a marriage candidate.

Set out orange water as an offering to the deities Hera and Juno for marriage and fidelity.

Orange Magical Properties:
Love, happiness, uplifting, generosity, purification, clarity, energy, fidelity.

Ruling planet – Sun
Element – Fire
Gender – Masculine

Oysters

A marine mollusc that can be eaten cooked or raw, personally I think a raw oyster tastes like a mouthful of salty snot, but that's just my personal view...

The oyster must be one of the most recognised foods as an aphrodisiac; the Romans loved an oyster and believed it was a very powerful source of sexual energy.

The oyster carries both masculine and feminine energies, so it brings balance and also stimulates the base chakra.

The shells are also very pretty and make lovely altar decorations or smudge and offering dishes.

Oyster Magical Properties:
Passion, balance.
Ruling planet – Moon
Element – Water
Gender – Masculine and feminine

Pancakes

Delicate lacy French crepes, thick squishy American stack pancakes or the ones we do at home where the first one always comes out like rubber and the rest never flip over properly... no matter how you eat them they are a definite comfort food, especially if served with heap loads of sugar or syrup.

With something like pancakes you take the magical properties of the ingredients, so you work with flour, milk and eggs. Add to those properties the all-round feelgood factor of pancakes themselves.

Papaya
(Carica papaya)

The papaya or paw paw is the fruit of the tropical *Carica papaya* tree, the flesh of the fruit is soft and the centre is filled with loads of black seeds. It is not a particular favourite of mine as I think the fruit tastes vaguely of feet...

To serve papaya to your loved one is said to increase their feelings of love or devotion to you. Unfortunately in my household where my husband dislikes fruit and I don't like papaya... I don't think it would be overly successful.

It is a very feminine fruit ruled by the moon and the element of water so this fruit is packed full of emotional energy.

Hanging the wood from a papaya tree over your doorways should bring about protection, but it is not an easy tree to get hold of unless you live in the tropical areas. You could, however, dry the seeds and use them in protection pouches instead.

Papaya Magical Properties:
Love, protection.
Ruling planet – Moon
Element – Water
Gender –Feminine

Paprika
(Capsicum annuum)

This lovely warm spice is made from dried chilli peppers. You can get mild and hot versions and also a very nice smoked paprika too.

Paprika brings a big punch of creative energy with it and can also be used as a 'booster' to other magical energies, either in your spell work or in your magical cooking.

As it has a chilli base you can also use it for protection. Sprinkle it around your house to keep out unwanted guests.

Paprika has a beautiful colour so it also makes a wonderful medium to use when drawing sigils or symbols for any magic work and can be included when making mandalas from natural items.

Paprika Magical Properties:
Creativity, energy.
Ruling planet – Mars
Element – Fire
Gender –Masculine

Parsley

(Petroselinum crispum, Petrselinum sativum)
Parsley was eaten to stop rowdiness and becoming drunk... you may have to test it yourself to find out if it works...

Rub parsley on your forehead, temple, then heart chakra with the intent of happiness and joy, then burn the parsley to ensure cheerfulness.

Be careful when in the party mood as parsley can also bring on lust and fertility... possibly not always a good combination.

Use parsley in incense blends to uplift and to purify the air. Drop a sprig of parsley into your bath water to cleanse your body from negative energy.

Carry parsley with you for personal protection and apparently that sad sprig of parsley on your plate in a restaurant as garnish is to protect food against contamination.

Parsley seems to have a lot of funereal ties and connections with the dead, so makes a good herb to use for otherworld and spirit work. It was also one of the ingredients often used in flying ointment.

Parsley Magical Properties:
Protection, purification, lust, happiness, fertility, spirit work.
Ruling planet – Mercury
Element – Air
Gender – Masculine

Parsnip

(Pastinaca sativa)

This root vegetable is related to the carrot and parsley. Parsnip is one of my favourite vegetables, in fact I prefer it to potatoes, especially roasted, and it also makes fabulous chips.

This veggie has a strong earthy and masculine energy so it works well in any kind of magic that requires a strong male energy; also in male sex magic workings.

Parsnip Magical Properties:
Male energy, sex magic.
Element – Earth
Gender – Masculine

Passion Fruit

(Passiflora edulis)

Now you would think that this fruit does what it says on the tin but it doesn't, well not exactly. What it does do is bring peace, calm, gentle love, friendship and all around good karma. However, it is a fruit ruled by Venus, the element of water and has feminine energies, so I would not dismiss it totally on the *ooh la la* front.

The passion flower got its name from missionaries who saw the flower as a symbol of the passion of Christ, likening the shape of the flower to the cross, the holy trinity, the crown of thorns and the 10 apostles (not including Judas or Peter). That's a lot of symbolism in one small flower!

Amazon (the place not the book store) natives used a variety of passion flower in their potions to help bring about visions.

Eat passion fruit to bring about calm and peace and also in any meals with your loved ones.

You could also try eating passion fruit before meditation or dream work.

It is the hippy karma of fruits that brings about your inner peace…. can we all chant 'ohmmm'.

Passion Fruit Magical Properties:
Love, peace, friendship, meditation, dreams.
Ruling planet – Venus
Element – Water
Gender – Feminine

Pasta

A good ol' kitchen cupboard staple that works brilliantly in culinary and magical ways as a base for magical additions (or sauces) and can also be used in a multitude of craft ways... to make necklaces and stick on picture frames (back to my childhood for a moment then).

Pasta is believed to have started life in Italy (of course) back in the 1300s.

Apparently pasta holds psychic energy and depending on the shape will dictate how much can be projected and stored in it, spaghetti being the weakest and shapes like tortellini and macaroni being the best... psychic pasta, how cool is that?

So, if you plan on doing any psychic work, eat a nice lasagne or cannelloni before you start.

Spiral shaped pasta should also help enhance your creativity and spaghetti or linguini will bring about personal protection and help improve communication. So if you aren't communicating with someone properly, serve up a big bowl of spaghetti.

Pasta Magical Properties:
Psychic powers, protection, communication, creativity.
Ruling planet – Mercury
Element – Earth
Gender – Masculine

Peach

(Prunus persica)
Such a feminine fruit jam packed with love, spiritual fertility and wishes just waiting to come true for you... awwww.

Serve up beautiful grilled peaches or a peach cobbler to your partner to win their love.

The peach tree when it is in blossom is also a sign of spring and purity.

In Asian culture the peach is also a sign of longevity.

Peach Magical Properties:
Love, fertility, spirituality, wishes, longevity.
Ruling planet – Venus
Element – Water, Air
Gender – Feminine

Peanut
(Arachis hypogaea)
The peanut or ground nut is actually a member of the legume family and it grows in quite an unusual way. After the flower is pollinated, the flower stalk bends to touch the ground and the continued growth of the stalk pushes it under the ground where the fruit develops in the peanut pod. Roasted 'monkey nuts' – the peanuts roasted still in their shell – are one of my favourite snacks.

The peanut has a huge amount of male energy; it is totally packed with 'he-man, kick sand in your face, body builder' kind of power.

Eat the peanuts for a big manly boost of energy or use the shells in spell work.

Roasted peanuts can also be eaten to increase the size of your... wallet (seriously what did you think I was going to say?). Peanut butter can be eaten for abundance too... not in abundance, that would just be greedy, but eat while visualising prosperity.

Peanut Magical Properties:
Masculine energy, prosperity.
Ruling planet – Jupiter
Element – Earth
Gender – Masculine

Pear

(Pyrus spp)

Oh what a lovely pear...

Sacred to the sacral chakra, associated with Venus the goddess of love, ruled by the planet Venus and the element of water, the humble pear is basically a fruit-filled passion machine.

During the Middle Ages eating a pear was believed to bring on passion and sexual arousal with immediate effect... so I would advise not eating one in the middle of the high street, it could be very embarrassing.

The pear is also another fruit believed to bring long life when eaten and also eaten for good luck and prosperity.

Pear Magical Properties:
Passion, love, prosperity, luck.
Ruling planet – Venus
Element – Water, Air
Gender – Feminine

Peas

(Pisum sativum)

Small, spherical green seeds from the *Pisum sativum* pod, a long description for a short word... pea.

The pea has got to be one of the smallest containers for love energy, but it is totally packed with it.

Peas are sacred to the mother goddesses.

Peas Magical Properties:
Love.
Ruling planet – Venus
Element – Water
Gender – Feminine

Pecan

(Carya illinoinensis)

The name pecan is apparently from an Algonquian word meaning a nut requiring a stone to crack... so that covers most nuts then...

You can't think about a pecan nut without deferring to the sumptuous pecan pie, all gooey and sweet... well I can't anyway... but all that nutty goodness helps make pecan pie a supreme champion in the magical money realm. Pecans are brilliant for prosperity and abundance. Also keep a pecan on your desk at work to ensure that you keep your job.

Pecan Magical Properties:
Prosperity.
Ruling planet – Mercury
Element – Air, Earth
Gender – Masculine

Pineapple

(Ananas comosus)

This has to be one of the weirdest looking fruits and one of the most difficult to 'peel', but it is delicious. It can be eaten fresh, cooked in sweet and savoury dishes and preserved.

The pineapple arrived in Europe during the 16th century and was thought to look like ... pine cone, well I guess it does really.

Drinking pineapple juice is said to ensure chastity (I have not tested this) and eating the fruit should bring you luck and prosperity. The pineapple can also be used in spell work for protection.

Eating pineapple can also aid in healing.

Pineapple Magical Properties:
Chastity, protection, luck, prosperity, healing.
Ruling planet – Sun

Element – Fire
Gender – Masculine

Pine nut

(Pinus spp)

The pine nut is an edible seed of the *Pinaceae* family, genus *Pinus*, so in fact not a nut at all, but a seed and has been served up as food since the Paleolithic period, but probably not toasted and sprinkled in a goats cheese salad then...

Use pine nuts in offerings to Bacchus, Neptune, Cybele and Pan.

Eat pine nuts to lift your mood, restore your strength and re-centre.

These little nuts are also brilliant to use in any kind of dragon magic.

The pine tree is one of protection so use the pine nuts to bring personal protection or sprinkle them around your property.

Pine nuts also bring the magical energy of hospitality so if you are having a dinner party use them in your menu to make your guests feel welcome.

Pine Nut Magical Properties:
Happiness, strength, centring, dragon magic, protection, hospitality.
Ruling planet – Mars, Saturn
Element – Air
Gender – Masculine

Pistachio

(Pistacia vera)

It made me laugh that this nut has a Latin name *'Vera'*... sounds quite friendly...

And while we are on the subject of silly names... Pliny the Elder suggested that pistachios were around in 6750BC and that

Lucius Viellius the Elder introduced them into Syria around 35 AD at the same time that Flaccus Pompeius brought them into Hispania... so many excellent names...

The pistachio is also mentioned in the Bible and archaeologists have found evidence of pistachio trees from 78,000 years ago. Basically this nut is old, very, very old.

These little alien-coloured (actually who knows if aliens are green?) nuts are a good ingredient to use for counteracting curses and hexes and also excellent to break love spells.

Eat pistachios to ground and centre yourself.

Pistachio shells also make good divination tools, hold them in your hand and give them a shake then scatter them on the deck, take a reading from where and how they fall.

Pistachio Magical Properties:
Hex breaking, grounding, divination.
Ruling planet – Mercury
Element – Earth, Air
Gender – Masculine

Plum
(Prunus spp)
There are heap loads of plum varieties and lots of different shades of colour. If you can get hold of the yellow plums they are especially delicious.

Serve plums to your loved one to attract them to you. The plum is also reputedly a very good aphrodisiac.

Eat plums and use the stones to increase your spiritual connection.

The Egyptians and Greeks used them to help relax the mind and the body.

The plum can be found in writings as early as 479BC. The plum tree is significant in Chinese myths and appeared frequently in the writings of Confucius.

The Chinese believe the plum to be a symbol of resurrection, longevity and great wisdom.

Plum Magical Properties:
Love, spirituality, relaxation, passion, longevity, wisdom, rebirth.
Ruling planet – Venus
Element – Water, Air
Gender – Feminine

Pomegranate
(Punica granatum)

My dad used to buy us a pomegranate each when we were children. He would give us the fruit and a pin to pick out the seeds; I suspect it was purely to keep us quiet for a bit...

The pomegranate always seems like a grand and extravagant fruit to me, maybe it is the colour of all the seeds inside. It is sacred to Persephone (the pomegranate appears in her stories) and Ceres and represents growth and fertility.

Eat pomegranate seeds while visualising your intent and if your will is strong enough your wish will come true.

This fruit is often associated with Samhain and the underworld (see the story of Persephone and Hades) so I think it works well for death and rebirth workings as well as new beginnings.

Pomegranate Magical Properties:
Growth, fertility, wishes, death, rebirth, new beginnings.
Ruling planet – Mercury
Element – Fire, Earth
Gender – Masculine

Poppy Seeds
(Papaver somniferum)

Poppy seeds come from the opium poppy, but don't get too

excited as they are the ripe seeds taken once the seed head has dried... the other sort, the ones that make your mind squiffy, are harvested when the pod is still green.

Poppy seeds can be eaten sprinkled on your meal to bring about a feeling of calm and peace.

The seeds are also often used as lucky talismans, sometimes dipped in gold first.

An old invisibility recipe says to soak poppy seeds in wine for 15 days and then drink the wine each day for five days while fasting... I would imagine it makes you fall over rather than become invisible!

The poppy flower has long been associated with witches and the wise woman and was said to be included in flying ointments.

Sprinkle the seeds around your property to confuse evil spirits and apparently to ward off vampires who feel impelled to stop and count them... I don't think vampires are that easily fooled...

The seeds are sacred to Hypnos, Nyx, Demeter and Persephone, who appreciate offerings of the seeds.

I also like to use poppy seeds for prosperity; they work very well in money spells.

Write a question that you might be pondering down on a slip of paper, roll it up with a poppy seed head inside and place it under your pillow. Hopefully the answer will appear in your dreams.

Poppy Seeds Magical Properties:
Calm, peace, luck, protection, invisibility, prosperity.
Ruling planet – Moon
Element – Air, Water
Gender – Feminine

Pork

This little piggy went to market...

I love pigs, having lived and worked on a pig farm in my youth I can appreciate firsthand what beautiful and intelligent creatures they are... although they can be seriously grumpy too...

Throughout history pork has been the meat of the poor man, the commoner if you will, so to me it has a great determined strength of energy to it.

The goddess Demeter kept a sacred pig, which became a symbol of fertility.

Native American Indians believe the pig to be a symbol of abundance and to be thankful for what life brings us.

The pig also appears in many cultures as a symbol of luck and prosperity.

The Celtic sea god Manannan had a herd of magical pigs, when eaten they imparted renewing qualities.

Pork Magical Properties:
Strength, fertility, prosperity, luck, longevity.
Element – Fire
Gender – Masculine

Potato

(Solanum tuberosum L)

The potato that we know and love in its many forms – mashed, roasted, baked, and chipped – is actually from the nightshade family...

Initially the potato got a lot of bad press and was believed to be poisonous, a carrier of infectious diseases and caused leprosy... I may never look at a chip in the same way again...

Gradually the potato found its way onto our plates and has become a staple food in our diet with a huge range of varieties, from little tiny purple new potatoes up to the huge baked potato.

The potato is a powerhouse of energy and also makes a very good poppet base.

Potato can be eaten in any form (I make a very nice lemon cake that has mashed potato in it) to help ground any excess energy.

The potato also works very well in prosperity and healing magic.

Potato Magical Properties:
Energy, magic, grounding, prosperity, healing.
Ruling planet – Moon
Element – Earth
Gender – Feminine

Pumpkin
(Cucurbita spp)
A pumpkin is for all year round, not just for Halloween…

There are a huge variety of pumpkins and all shapes, colours and sizes, which can be used in savoury and sweet dishes.

Obviously the pumpkin has a Samhain connection and I think with that comes the crone association as well, so it works well in any celebration or honouring dish for either.

Pumpkin seeds not only make a yummy snack, they also work brilliantly in prosperity magic.

Bake pumpkin into pies and casseroles to bring abundance and money to your life. I also think the pumpkin has fabulous healing properties too… a big ol' slice of pumpkin pie sure makes me feel better anyway.

Pumpkin Magical Properties:
Prosperity, crone magic, healing.
Ruling planet – Moon
Element – Earth
Gender – Feminine

Quince
(Cydonia oblonga)
Quite an old fashioned fruit, quince is not one that you will find very often in the shops, but I can remember going scrumping

with my grandmother to get them to make into quince jelly.

The quince is a deciduous tree that bears fruit that looks a bit similar to the apple and pear, but is bright yellow when ripe. The tree is worth growing just for the blossom, which is a lovely pink colour.

The quince is actually part of the *Roseacea* family so it brings with it the magical properties of love and happiness.

The quince is sacred to the goddess Venus, or Aphrodite.

Romans would serve quince to their loved ones to encourage fidelity and those newly married would share a quince to ensure a happy marriage.

In ancient Greece a bride would eat a piece of quince to 'perfume her kiss' before she entered the bridal chamber... a forerunner to the breath mint I guess.

The Roman philosopher Pliny (the Elder) believed the quince to be a fruit that warded against evil.

The flesh is fairly bitter, so the quince is best eaten cooked and works well in jelly, jam and preserves, but also in chutneys and pies.

Quince Magical Properties:
Love, happiness, fidelity, protection.
Ruling planet – Saturn
Element – Earth
Gender – Feminine

Radish

(Raphanus sativus)
The radish is a root vegetable from the *Brassicaceae* family that comes in all sorts of shapes, sizes and colours, each of them packing a fiery punch. Usually eaten raw, the radish is also quite nice cooked.

The Greeks and Romans spoke of radishes in the 1st century AD.

The radish brings protection from the Evil Eye, so eat plenty for personal protection.

Also eat radish to stimulate the sacral chakra and to power up your sexual energy.

This veggie grows very quickly so it makes a good seed spell to rid yourself of any worries or troubles. Plant a few radish seeds on your windowsill (in a pot first obviously) send all your troubles into the seeds, then watch them grow; as they grow they will transform your problems into new life and bring happiness and positive energy into your home.

Radish Magical Properties:
Protection, passion, happiness.
Ruling planet – Mars
Element – Fire
Gender – Masculine

Raspberry
(Rubus spp.)
One of my favourite fruits, the raspberry is soft and sweet, usually red in colour, but you can also get golden yellow, blue, purple and black varieties.

Raspberry juice is excellent to drink or use in ritual and spell work to provide protection.

The raspberry is also a brilliant fruit of love and can be eaten or used in workings to bring about that 'lurve thang'.

Raspberries make a wonderful offering for the goddess Aphrodite and also to Hecate and Isis.

It is said that this small squishy berry induces stamina and vigour.

Raspberry leaves can also be used to make herbal tea.

Raspberry Magical Properties:
Love, protection, strength.

Ruling planet – Venus
Element – Water, Earth
Gender – Feminine

Relish, Chutney, Pickle

Any type of relish, pickle or chutney has taken a while to make and mature so it stands to reason that it will enhance the magical properties of the ingredients used.

Rhubarb

(Rheum rhabarbarum)

Although we use rhubarb mainly in sweet dishes it is classed as a vegetable.

Rhubarb is said to increase your willpower and reduce worry... right I'm gonna need truckloads of the stuff then...

Serve rhubarb to your lover to place them under your power (I feel the need to cackle *mwhahahaaaa* at this point).

Rhubarb was used during the great plague for protection against the Black Death, so it works well for protective magical use; the dried leaves ground up would make a good ingredient in witches' bottles or medicine pouches.

Rhubarb Magical Properties:
Willpower, worry, love, protection.
Ruling planet – Venus
Element – Earth
Gender – Feminine

Rice

(Oryza spp)

A cereal grain, rice must be one of the main staple foods eaten across the world and it comes in lots of varieties: long grain, short grain, pudding, basmati, risotto, black, red... you name it, they got it.

Rice is one of the Seven Sacred Grains, the others being barley, corn, oats, millet, rye and wheat. These grains are responsible for keeping cultures, entire civilisations and, indeed, mankind alive.

We throw rice at weddings to bring fertility and abundance to the happy couple.

I use rice a lot in spell work to symbolise money and prosperity, but it also works really well in witches' bottles to 'soak up' negative energy and provide protection.

To add some money-bringing oomph to your rice it needs to come in contact with currency, so drop a few silver coins into your box of rice or roll up a note or two and pop it in there.

Colouring your rice dishes with green food colouring will also increase the money-making energy.

Rice is also said to be good for bringing rain... but as I live in the UK where we have more rain than we need I haven't tested this.

Try mixing some glitter into your dried rice to add to prosperity medicine pouches... you can never have enough glitter... but don't eat it...

Keeping a jar of rice near your front door is said to distract evil spirits as they are compelled to stop in the doorway to count the grains, thus protecting your home.

Rice makes a good grounding meal, bringing stability and comfort with it.

Rice Magical Properties:
Prosperity, fertility, protection, rain, grounding, stability.
Ruling planet – Sun
Element – Air, Earth
Gender – Masculine

Rosemary
(Rosemarinus officinalis)
This is a popular herb found in many gardens (apparently introduced to the UK by the Romans), I have several in mine and it

grows all year round.

An evergreen plant, it has woody stems, narrow dark green leaves and tiny lilac colour flowers that bloom twice a year, once in the spring and again in the autumn. The whole plant is aromatic and has a habit of covering you in strongly scented oil whenever you handle the leaves.

Greeks wore rosemary in their hair to help boost the power of memory.

Traditionally rosemary was burnt as incense in houses that were stricken with illness; I like to also use it in my smudge sticks along with lavender and sage.

Grow, carry with you or use in incense blends to bring about protection, healing and purification.

It was often used in bridal bouquets for love and funeral wreaths for remembrance.

Use a long piece of fresh rosemary and bend it into a circle, tie it together with ribbon and hang it in your home to bring protection.

Burning rosemary as incense in your home apparently gets rid of unwanted guests or those who have outstayed their welcome.

I have read that folklore states rosemary will only flourish in the garden where the lady rules the house... (it grows really well in my garden)...

Rosemary Magical Properties:
Protection, love, lust, mental powers, exorcism, purification, healing, sleep.
Ruling planet – Sun
Element – Fire
Gender – Masculine

Rye
(Secale cereal)
A grain crop, rye is mainly used in cooking to make bread. It is

highly susceptible to the ergot fungus, consumption of which can cause serious health problems both mentally and physically. It has been suggested that the women accused of being possessed during the Salem witch trials in 1692 were actually suffering from ergotism after eating infected rye.

Rye is another one of the Seven Sacred Grains.

Rye is often baked into bread to give to a lover to increase their feelings for the giver, but I would suggest adding rye to your diet to increase self love too.

Rye Magical Properties:
Love.
Ruling planet – Venus
Element – Earth
Gender – Feminine

Saffron
(Crocus sativus)

Saffron comes from the dried stigmas of the *crocus sativus*, it is expensive, but produces a lovely flavour and an amazing golden yellow colour to your food.

Saffron appears in all sorts of mythology and history; Cleopatra was said to add saffron to her bath to make lovemaking more pleasurable (well obviously she didn't add it, one of her servants would have done) and saffron was used in perfumes by the ancient Egyptians and Greeks and also used as a fabric dye. One legend tells the story of Crocus and Smilax where Crocus is bewitched and transformed into the first saffron crocus, another story tells of Hermes who accidentally wounded his friend Crocus, where the blood dripped onto the earth the crocus flower grew.

Eating a dish with saffron in will dispel depression and increase your motivation. Although it was once believed that eating too much of it could cause death from excessive joy…

Drinking saffron tea can help increase both your psychic and healing powers.

Saffron is sacred to the Egyptian god Amen and the Greek god Eos.

Carry a pouch of saffron with you if you are pregnant to help ensure a safe pregnancy and birth, saffron also brings the magical energy of fertility.

However you eat saffron or work with it, this spice has the colour and essence of sunshine and is most definitely a very happy ingredient.

Saffron Magical Properties:
Happiness, energy, psychic powers, healing, fertility.
Ruling planet – Sun
Element – Fire
Gender – Masculine

Sage
(Salvia officinalis)
A familiar herb in our gardens, I have the garden/common variety and a pretty purple sage too. It is an evergreen perennial shrub with woody stems and grey leaves (unless you have the purple or variegated varieties) with small lilac coloured flowers.

The white sage (*Salvia apiana*) that is traditionally used for smudging by many American tribes is native to the USA and Mexico. Personally I use the sage that grows in my garden to smudge because it is very similar, I also know that it is free of pesticides and chemicals and I get it for free.

Carry sage with you to ensure wisdom and aid with your intuition.

To cleanse, purify and protect your home, work or ritual space, smudge with sage, although I like to add rosemary and lavender into my smudge bundles.

Keep sage on your windowsill or add to your recipes to

encourage abundance and success.

Write your wish on a sage leaf and place it beneath your pillow; if you dream of your goal then it will come true.

Sage is sacred to the gods Zeus and Jupiter and to the Virgin Mary.

Sage also stimulates the throat chakra.

Sage Magical Properties:
Protection, wishes, wisdom, purification, stimulating, intuition, abundance, success.
Ruling planet – Jupiter
Element – Air
Gender – Masculine

Salt

Salt is a very common ingredient, but also a very powerful magical one. And yes I know we are supposed to reduce our salt intake, but food just doesn't taste the same if it hasn't been seasoned, so just be frugal with it.

Salt is sacred to the Egyptian gods Osiris and Set.

It is cleansing, purifying and protective.

It has a strong female energy. Alchemists believed it to be the opposite of sulphur, which has the male energy.

In European folk magic and Hoodoo it is common practice to sprinkle a pinch of salt in each corner of the room before starting any spell work.

Salt on its own is very protective, but mix it with any kind of pepper – black, red or cayenne – and you get a much stronger mix.

Black salt or Witches' Salt is a mixture of salt (what a surprise) and charcoal with sometimes black pepper added and is used for both good magic and darker magic. It can be used to throw behind an enemy so that they move away or sprinkled in their garden to get rid of them, but black salt is also incredibly good at providing personal protection.

Salt can also be added to bath water (Epsom salt is best for this) to purify and cleanse before ritual or to get rid of negative energy.

Sprinkling salt on your food will also provide protection.

I think it is probably illegal to eat potato fries without salt…

Salt Magical Properties:
Cleansing, purification, protection.
Ruling planet – Earth
Element – Earth
Gender – Feminine

Sausages

Sausages, burgers, kebabs and hot dogs bring with them the magical powers of the animal from which they are made, along with any herbs that have been added. They are definitely a strong male energy though.

Sesame

(Sesamum indicum)

Sesame seeds come from a pod that grows on the *Sesamum indicum* plant. We use the seeds and the oil in cooking.

The sesame seed is sacred to the Hindu god Lord Ganesha and they are eaten to increase and strengthen your inner life force, the energy that comes from your kundalini, your base chakra. They are also sacred to the goddess Hecate.

It was believed that sesame plants grew next to secret entrances and hidden pathways to the unknown perhaps that is where the magical command 'open sesame' comes from.

In the Assyrian creation myth it is said that the gods drank sesame wine the night before they created the world… so basically they did it with a huge hangover.

Eating sesame seeds is believed to increase your *va va voom* and also fertility.

Eat or use sesame seeds in spell work for prosperity and money drawing.

The seeds can also be used in protection workings.

Sesame Magical Properties:
Prosperity, protection, energy, strength, secrets.
Ruling planet – Sun
Element – Fire, Earth
Gender – Masculine

Soup

Another 'carrier', soup brings out the energies of the ingredients used.

Soup is sacred to the goddess Cerridwen and aligns with the element of water.

Soya Bean

(Glycine max)

The soya bean comes from the legume family and is used in cooking, as soya milk or made into tofu and fermented into soy sauce or bean paste. I cook a lot with soya milk and soy sauce, but I have to admit I would rather eat a bath sponge than tofu… same texture, but I think the bath sponge probably tastes better…

Any soya product works well for fertility and to increase your sexual desire.

Soya is sacred to the Japanese deities Ebisu and Daikotu who prepare tofu and to Japanese harvest deities.

In Japanese culture soya beans are symbols of abundance, good luck and protection.

Eat tofu to increase your psychic abilities and to strengthen your spiritual connection.

Soya Bean Magical Properties:
Fertility, passion, prosperity, luck, psychic powers, spirituality.

Ruling planet – Moon
Element – Earth
Gender – Feminine

Spinach
(Spinacia oleracea)
The baby leaves of spinach are yummy in salads, the larger older leaves are best cooked and frozen. Spinach works very well in all sorts of recipes.

It is another vegetable that brings heap loads of sexual energy and fertility (seriously how do we get through the day without jumping on each other?)

Spinach also has a huge amount of energy and strength... just like Popeye.

Spinach Magical Properties:
Passion, fertility, strength.
Ruling planet – Jupiter
Element – Earth
Gender – Feminine

Squash
See pumpkin.

Star Anise
(Illicum verum)
An ancient herb, the star-shape seeds of star anise come from an evergreen shrub and the seedpods are picked just before the fruit ripens and are dried in the sun. The star shape of the seed lends itself to all sorts of magical correspondences and representations. They have a delicious aniseed aroma and taste.

Place star anise in the corner of each room in your home to bring luck. Keep a whole star anise on your altar to help keep a spiritual connection. Place a star anise beneath your pillow to induce prophetic dreams and also to help you sleep.

Burn star anise as an incense to purify and protect your home and also to help increase your psychic powers, or wear one in an amulet or pouch to provide psychic protection and keep away evil.

Make a sachet of star anise and bay to pop into your bathwater to purify and cleanse your aura and energies.

It is also a good herb to use in new moon rituals and spell work along with new moon recipe dishes.

Star Anise Magical Properties:

Luck, psychic powers, purification, protection, dreams, spirituality, sleep.

Ruling planet – Jupiter

Element – Air

Gender – Masculine

Strawberry

(Fragaria spp)

One of THE main love fruits, especially when dipped in chocolate… although during the 1600s it was customary to dip them in wine before eating.

Strawberries are sacred to the fertility god Freyr and carry that magical energy along with love and romance. They also work well in honouring Frigg, Freya, Aphrodite and the Virgin Mary.

Strawberry leaves work really well in workings for good luck and success.

Strawberry Magical Properties:

Love, fertility, romance, luck, success.

Ruling planet – Venus

Element – Water, Earth

Gender – Feminine

Sugar

The stuff that makes life sweet, which is exactly how I use it magically. I add it to witches' bottles, medicine pouches and sachet powders to add a little life sweetener.

Sugar is ruled by Venus and the element of water so it makes a good ingredient for love workings and recipes.

Sacred to the Hawaiian god Kane, sugar is used to rid evil and works very well for protection.

Sugar Magical Properties:
Love, protection.
Ruling planet – Venus
Element – Water
Gender – Feminine

Sunflower Seeds

(Helianthus annuus)
The sunflower seeds come from the *Helianthus annuus* plant, but what we eat as a snack or in recipes is actually the kernel of the seed once it has been dehulled.

The sunflower is sacred to the Greek deities Helios, Demeter and Apollo and is associated with the crown chakra.

The seeds carry a powerful masculine energy and should be eaten by ladies who wish to become pregnant.

The Aztecs used sunflowers to decorate their temples and the priestesses wore them in their hair. The petals can also be used to make a dye.

The sunflower has strong sun energy, which is not really surprising! This brings the magical properties of strength, confidence and courage along with a bright sunshiny happy energy.

Sunflower seeds also work well in prosperity rituals and workings and recipes.

Sunflower Seeds Magical Properties:
Fertility, sun magic, strength, courage, happiness, prosperity, confidence.
Ruling planet – Sun
Element – Fire
Gender – Masculine

Swede
(Rutabaga/Brassica napus)
See turnip.

Sweet Potato
(Ipomoea batatas)
The sweet potato is a large, sweet tasting root vegetable. It makes a lovely sweet mash or the most amazing chips.

The sweet potato for me is comforting and nurturing and real 'wrapped up in a big hug' kinda food. I think it works well in offerings to any of the mother goddesses.

The sweet potato also carries a strong love vibe from the gentle love of friendship right through to the passionate 'let's take our clothes off' energy... don't get them mixed up... it is all down to your intent.

Sweet Potato Magical Properties:
Love, passion.
Ruling planet – Venus
Element – Earth, Water
Gender – Feminine

Tea
(Camellia sinensis)
A good ol' cup of tea (see earlier chapter, The Magic of Tea).

Your tea leaves are not only good for divination they also hold excellent magical properties. Tea is ruled by the sun and the element of fire so it packs a huge powerful punch of magical energy.

Tea is lovely to drink before meditation, helping you relax and let go of your worries.

Tea leaves can be used in all kinds of magical workings to bring about courage, strength and prosperity.

Tea Magical Properties:
Meditation, courage, strength, prosperity.
Ruling planet – Sun
Element – Fire
Gender – Masculine

Thyme
(Thymus vulgaris, Thymus serpyllum)
A low growing woody herb with small green leaves and tiny lilac coloured flowers throughout the summer, this herb smells and tastes delicious. Wild thyme can be found growing in woods, fields, and commons and on heathlands.

It is an excellent herb to use in any healing workings and in culinary use for healing too.

Burn in incense blends or carry with you for good health. Also use it in incense blends to purify and cleanse your home and bring love and peace in.

Thyme will increase your willpower and give you courage.

Making (and drinking) thyme tea will help you release the past; you can also add the tea mix to your bath water.

Sleep with thyme under your pillow to ensure you sleep soundly and mix thyme with lavender to make a brilliant sleep pillow.

Romans would wash their faces in thyme water to enhance their attractiveness and carry it with them to ward off venomous creatures.

Thyme Magical Properties:

Healing, health, peace, psychic powers, love, purification, courage, releasing, sleep, beauty.

Ruling planet – Venus

Element – Water

Gender – Feminine

Tomato

(Solanum lycopersicum)

There are so many varieties of the tomato from tiny cherry ones to huge beefsteaks and all sorts of wonderful colours.

The tomato has often been referred to as the 'love apple' so in that regard, along with being ruled by Venus and water, it works well in all recipes and meals to share with a loved one. The seeds can also be dried and used in love spell work. I say use the seeds because using a tomato in a medicine pouch would be terribly squishy and messy...

The tomato is sacred to Venus, Aphrodite and Hera.

Keep a tomato on your windowsill to stop negative energy from entering your home.

Eating tomatoes inspires love and passion, but also creativity.

Tomato Magical Properties:

Love, passion, protection, creativity.

Ruling planet – Venus

Element – Water

Gender – Feminine

Turkey

This is a bird that we only usually seem to eat on holidays amidst problems trying to fit it in the oven and the amount of time it takes to cook.

It is a proud and powerful bird and carries the magical properties of motivation, clarity and focus.

The feathers also make excellent smudging tools.

Turkey Magical Properties:
Motivation, clarity, focus, celebration.
Element – Fire, Air
Gender – Masculine

Turmeric
(Cucurma longa)
Turmeric is a perennial plant with long tuberous roots; it is this part that is used to make the spice we are familiar with.

Dissolve turmeric and salt in water to make a blessing and purifying liquid to sprinkle around your home, workplace or ritual area. Be careful as turmeric does stain, unless you want everything to turn bright yellow...

Put a piece of turmeric root above your threshold to protect your home.

Use turmeric in incense blends to purify and bring peace to your house.

Turmeric Magical Properties:
Purification, protection, peace.
Ruling planet – Mars
Element – Fire, Air
Gender – Feminine

Turnip
(Brassica rapa var. rapa)
The turnip or white turnip is a spherical root vegetable that was the original 'carved pumpkin'. The turnips were carved out and a candle placed inside to scare off evil spirits on Halloween. The flesh of the turnip is a lot harder than that of a pumpkin so carving must have been a major feat.

Serve turnips to someone who you wish would leave you alone.

In Scotland and the north of England the turnip (or neep) refers to the larger more yellow in colour root vegetable, the swede (Swedish turnip), but they carry the same magical properties.

Turnip Magical Properties:
Protection.
Element – Earth
Gender – Masculine

Vanilla
(Vanilla planifolia)
Vanilla seeds come from an orchid in the vanilla family. The seeds are scraped from the vanilla pod to use as flavouring and the pod can then be saved and used to flavour alcohol (gin and rum work well, just drop the pod into the bottle) or popped into your sugar box to flavour the sugar.

Vanilla can be used to increase love and happiness whether it is in your cooking or spell work. The vanilla beans can also help to increase your spirituality and connection to a higher level of consciousness.

The scent of vanilla can be used for any love and sex magic to attract a lover or to increase levels of passion. It can also be used to spark your imagination and creativity.

Vanilla Magical Properties:
Love, spirituality, sex magic, passion, creativity.
Ruling planet – Venus
Element – Water, Air
Gender – Feminine

Vinegar
(Acetic acid/water)
Any type of vinegar can be used to add the element of fire to your dishes or spell work. It is also an ingredient in the Four Thieves

Vinegar used in Hoodoo for protection and getting rid of enemies.

Vinegar Magical Properties:
Fire energy, protection.
Ruling planet – Mars
Element – Fire
Gender – Masculine

Walnut
(Juglans regia)
The walnut is a tall sturdy tree with a large canopy; small flowers are followed by the walnut fruit, which ripens in September.

Work with the energy of walnut to help increase your mental clarity and help with decision making.

Sleep with a walnut under your bed to increase fertility.

Use walnut shells as 'holders'; write your wishes on small pieces of paper and pop them inside a walnut shell, bury or burn them to set the intent of your wishes.

Walnut Magical Properties:
Wishes, mental powers, clarity, fertility.
Ruling planet – Sun
Element – Fire
Gender – Masculine

Water
Water ... a necessity of life.

Used in all sorts of cooking, recipes and to drink, it is a total life source of power.

Ruled by the moon, water is a carrier for emotions, but also cleansing and purifying.

Make your own moon water by leaving out a dish of distilled water under any phase of the moon (full, waning, waxing, and dark) to create a magical water to use in spell work.

Make crystal water by leaving a crystal in a bottle or dish of distilled water so that the magical properties of the crystal impart into the water. Please be careful to use a crystal that is not going to be damaged by soaking in water, or one that is toxic, and remember to remove the crystal before you drink the water.

Water Magical Properties:
Emotions, cleansing, purification.
Ruling planet – Moon
Element – Water
Gender – Feminine

Watercress
(Nasturtium officinale)
Watercress was favoured by the ancient Greeks and Romans who believed that it brought clarity and strength to the mind.

Watercress brings a huge whack of feminine energy with it.

Watercress as the name suggests grows by the water and has the magical properties of protection and also fertility.

Use it in salads and soups.

Watercress Magical Properties:
Clarity, protection, fertility.
Ruling planet – Mars
Element – Fire, Water
Gender – Feminine

Wheat
(Triticum spp.)
This is the cereal grain that appears in a huge amount of our foods.

One of the Seven Sacred Grains and the one that represents abundance, prosperity and rebirth.

Wheat is sacred to Ishtar, Osiris, Demeter and Ceres. It is a symbol of the harvest, the mother goddess and the bounty that the earth provides for us.

Eat bread and recipes made from wheat to bring prosperity and abundance into your life.

Bread also lends itself to being a carrier for any magical intent. While you are making the bread visualise your desire and send that energy into the dough. You could even mark a symbol in the top of the bread to correspond with your intent before you bake it.

Wheat Magical Properties:
Prosperity, rebirth, abundance, wishes.
Ruling planet – Venus
Element – Earth
Gender – Feminine

Wine

Just one more glass...

Wine is scared to Dionysus, Bacchus, Osiris, Horus and Isis, but it makes a very good offering to most deities.

Wine is believed to contain the spirit of happiness and divine love... unless you drink way too much then you love everyone in the whole world.

Wine for me has a very spiritual connection; pretty much every monastery would have had its own brew of wine, beer or mead.

Wine Magical Properties:
Spirituality, offerings, happiness, love.
Ruling planet – Sun (red wine), Moon (white wine)
Element – Earth, Fire
Gender – Masculine and Feminine

Yogurt

A fermented milk product that has quite a spiritual energy and one of inspiration and creativity, I also think yogurt will carry not only the magical properties of milk, but also those of the animal that provided the milk, whether it is a cow or a goat or that yak we mentioned…

In the 16th century it was apparently used to treat depression.

Yogurt Magical Properties:
Spirituality, creativity, depression.
Ruling planet – Moon
Element – Water, Air
Gender – Feminine

Correspondence Charts

Here I have broken down all the information given in the previous chapter into hopefully handy correspondence charts. These charts show at-a-glance correspondences, but as always go with your own personal intuition. These are just a guide, there is no right or wrong food, herb or plant to use.

Planet Characteristics

Moon – Emotions, intuition, divination, spirituality, cleansing, purity, unity, prosperity, psychic abilities, magic, change, feminine energy, the goddess, personality, desires and cycles.

Mars – Passion, vitality, primal, aggression, motivation, strength, energy, sex, masculine energy, ambition, assertiveness, power, achievement, ROAR!

Mercury – Communication, confidence, acceptance, knowledge, adaptability, self expression, travel, skill and learning.

Jupiter – Influence, luck, prosperity, career, accomplishment, fulfilment, attainment, growth, opportunity, health and finances.

Venus – Love, lust, romance, fertility, money, healing, friendships, family, emotional attachments, hope, feminine energies, sharing, charm, grace.

Saturn – Renewal, changes, boundaries, restrictions, obstacles, protection, loss, blocking, holding, binding, the law, limitations, interruptions, returning and ambition.

Sun – Success, empowerment, ambition, enlightenment, goals, generosity, spirituality, male energies, health, vitality, the god, material wealth, pride, individuality and energy.

Intent Correspondence Chart

Anti Theft – Cumin

Astral Travel – Mustard

Bad Habits – Chives

Balance – Liquorice, mushroom, oysters

Beauty – Avocado, beetroot, thyme

Beginnings – Cherry, eggs, lamb, pomegranate

Binding – Maple syrup

Calming – Blueberry, gravy, lettuce, mint, poppy seeds

Centring – Pine nut

Changes – Cinnamon

Chaos – Melon

Chastity – Coconut, cucumber, pineapple

Clarity – Apple, bergamot, cardamom, carrot, celery, clove, coffee, mustard, orange, rosemary, turkey, walnut, watercress

Celebration – Cake, turkey

Cleansing – Asparagus, fish, gravy, mint, salt, water

Communication – Cranberry, pasta

Confidence – Black pepper, sunflower seed

Courage – Artichoke, garlic, liver, lobster, mushroom, sunflower seed, tea, thyme

Creation – Eggs

Creativity – Bay, chillies, paprika, pasta, tomato, vanilla, yogurt

Decisions – Lemon

Depression (anti) – Garlic, grapefruit, yogurt

Divination – Bean, cherry, chicken, coffee, eggs, figs, game, lemongrass, pistachio

Dragon magic – Pine nut

Dreams – Beer, jasmine, lettuce, passion fruit, star anise

Emotions – Cauliflower, caviar, cranberry, cucumber, fish, gravy, water

Endurance – Brussels sprouts

Energy – Baking powder, cashew, chillies, coffee, curry, game, grapefruit, horseradish, lime, orange, paprika, potato, saffron, sesame

Exorcism – Basil, black pepper, chives, clove, cumin, mint, rosemary

Faerie – Blackberries, butter, hazelnut, honey, lemongrass, milk

Fertility – Avocado, beef, blackberry, blueberry, cabbage, carrot, cherry, chestnut, chicken, corn, cucumber, eggs, elderflower, figs, fish, grapes, hazelnut, lamb, lettuce, mango, oats, olives, onions, parsley, peach, pomegranate, pork, rice, soya, spinach, strawberry, sunflower seed, walnut, watercress

Fidelity – Cumin, game, lemon, nutmeg, orange, quince, saffron

Focus – Cinnamon, turkey

Friendship – Lemon, passion fruit

Generosity – Orange

Goddess Energy – Milk, pumpkin

Gossip (stopping & preventing) – Black pepper, clove

Grounding – Barley, beetroot, borage, bread, cake, cookies, pistachio, potato, rice

Growth – Artichoke, sunflower, pomegranate

Happiness – Basil, cake, lavender, cheese, chocolate, grapefruit, honey, jelly, lemon, lemongrass, marjoram, orange, parsley, pine nut, quince, radish, saffron, sunflower seed, wine

Healing – Apple, asparagus, barley, bay, carnation, chicken, cinnamon, coriander, cucumber, fennel, fish, garlic, ginger, gravy, hazelnut, honey, lime, maple syrup, marjoram, melon, mint, olives, pineapple, potato, pumpkin, rose, rosemary, saffron, thyme

Hex breaking – Chillies, crab, garlic, pistachio

Hospitality – Pine nut

Intuition – Almond

Jealousy – Black pepper

Longevity – Peach, plum, pork

Love – Almond, apple, apricot, avocado, barley, basil, beetroot, brazil nut, cabbage, cardamom, cherry, chocolate, cinnamon, clove, clover, coriander, cumin, daisy, endive, figs, ginger, guava, honey, ice cream, jasmine, kiwi fruit, lavender, leeks, lemon, lime, liquorice, mango, maple syrup, marjoram, melon, milk, nasturtium, nectarine, orange, pansy, papaya, passion fruit, peach, pear, peas, plum, quince, raspberry, rhubarb, rose, rosemary, rye, strawberry, sugar, sweet potato, tomato, vanilla, wine

Luck – Chicken, corn, kumquat, nutmeg, olives, pear, pineapple, poppy seeds, pork, soya, star anise, strawberry

Magic – Baking powder, mushroom, potato

Meditation – Cucumber, figs, lettuce, passion fruit, tea

Moon magic – Cabbage, cauliflower, grapes, lemon, milk

Motivation – Turkey

Negativity (dispelling) – Black pepper, chives, clove, coriander, garlic, sunflower

Nurturing – Lamb, milk

Offerings – Beer, bread, cake, corn, cornmeal, dates, milk, wine

Passion/lust – Almond, apricot, artichoke, asparagus, avocado, beetroot, blueberry, cardamom, carrot, caviar, celery, chillies, cinnamon, cumin, curry, daisy, endive, garlic, ginger, honey, horseradish, liquorice, mango, nasturtium, oats, pansy, olives, onions, oysters, parsley, pear, plum, radish, rosemary, soya, spinach, sweet potato, tomato, vanilla

Peace – Blueberry, butter, celery, coriander, cumin, olives, passion fruit, poppy seeds, thyme, turmeric

Positive Energy – Chocolate, maple syrup

Power – Baking powder, bay, beef, chillies, cinnamon, game, ginger, liver, lobster

Prosperity/money/wealth/abundance – Almond, apple, aubergine, banana, basil, bean, bergamot, blackberry, brazil nut, cabbage, cashew, chamomile, chestnut, chicken, chocolate, clove, clover, coriander, corn, cumin, elderflower, fish, ginger, honey, jasmine, kumquat, macadamia, maple syrup, mint, nasturtium, nutmeg, oats, peanut, pear, pecan, pineapple, poppy seeds, pork, potato, pumpkin, rice, sage, sesame, soya, sunflower seed, tea, wheat

Psychic powers – Almond, bay, cinnamon, hazelnut, mustard, pasta, saffron, sage, soya, star anise, thyme

Protection – Artichoke, barley, basil, bay, blackberry, black pepper, blueberry, broccoli, Brussels sprouts, cabbage, cardamom, carnation, cauliflower, chamomile, chillies, chives, chrysanthemum, cinnamon, clove, clover, coconut, coriander, cranberry, cumin, curry leaves, elderflower, fennel, garlic, ginger, hazelnut, horseradish, lavender, leeks, lemon, lilac, lime, marjoram, mint, mustard, nutmeg, olives, papaya, parsley, pasta, pineapple, pine nut, poppy seeds, quince, radish, raspberry, rhubarb, rice, rose, rosemary, sage, salt, sesame, star anise, sugar, tomato, turmeric, turnip, vinegar, watercress

Purification – Bay, beer, coconut, cucumber, fennel, fish, grapefruit, gravy, guava, horseradish, lavender, leeks, lemon, lime, melon, orange, parsley, rosemary, sage, salt, star anise, thyme, turmeric, water

Rebirth – Dates, plum, pomegranate, wheat

Relaxation – Plum

Release – Coriander, thyme

Ritual – Cake, cookies, lemongrass

Rites of Passage – Cake

Romance – Apricot, guava, kiwi fruit, strawberry

Secrets – Sesame

Sex – Asparagus, parsnip, vanilla

Shape shifting – Lemongrass

Sleep – Rosemary, star anise, thyme

Spirit work – Apple, grapefruit, parsley

Spirituality – Banana, bay, butter, cinnamon, crab, cucumber, dates, grapes, honey, ice cream, mango, milk, mustard, olives, peach, plum, soya, star anise, vanilla, wine, yogurt

Stability – Brussels sprouts, rice

Strength – Artichoke, bay, black pepper, broccoli, chestnut, garlic, mushroom, pine nut, pork, raspberry, sesame, spinach, sunflower seed, tea

Stress relief – Clove, rhubarb

Success – Bergamot, borage, cheese, chestnut, cinnamon, cumin, ginger, mustard, sage, strawberry

Support – Borage

Truth – Clove

Uplifting – Cardamom, lemon, orange

Wisdom/knowledge – Apple, bean, hazelnut, lemongrass, plum, sage

Willpower – Rhubarb

Wishes – Peach, pomegranate, sage, walnut, wheat

Planet Correspondence Chart

Earth – Salt

Jupiter – Asparagus, aubergine, chestnut, clove, endive, figs, grapefruit, macadamia, maple syrup, nutmeg, peanut, sage, spinach, star anise

Mars – Artichoke, asparagus, banana, basil, beer, black pepper, cardamom, carrot, chillies, chives, chocolate, coffee, coriander, cranberry, cumin, curry, curry leaves, garlic, ginger, horseradish, leeks, mango, mustard, onions, paprika, pine nut, radish, turmeric, vinegar, watercress

Mercury – Almond, bean, celery, fennel, hazelnut, lemongrass, liquorice, marjoram, mint, parsley, pasta, pecan, pistachio, pomegranate

Moon – Blueberry, broccoli, Brussels sprouts, butter, cabbage, cauliflower, caviar, coconut, crab, cucumber, grapes, gravy, ice cream, kiwi fruit, lemon, lettuce, melon, milk, mushroom, oyster, papaya, poppy seeds, potato, pumpkin, soya, water, white wine, yogurt

Saturn – Beetroot, cheese, pine nut, quince

Sun – Bay, cashew, cinnamon, corn, dates, grapefruit, hazelnut, kumquat, lime, olives, orange, pineapple, rice, rosemary, saffron, sesame, sunflower seed, tea, walnut, red wine

Venus – Apple, apricot, avocado, barley, blackberry, brazil nut, cardamom, cherry, liquorice, mint, nectarine, oats, passion fruit, peach, pear, peas, plum, raspberry, rhubarb, rye, strawberry, sugar, sweet potato, thyme, tomato, vanilla, wheat

Element Correspondence Chart

Earth – Avocado, aubergine, barley, beetroot, blackberry, blueberry, brazil nut, bread, butter, cake, cashew, cheese, corn, eggs, flour, game, honey, kiwi fruit, liquorice, macadamia, maple syrup, mushroom, oats, parsnip, pasta, peanut, pecan, pistachio, pomegranate, potato, pumpkin, quince, raspberry, rhubarb, rice, rye, salt, sesame, soya, spinach, strawberry, sweet potato, turnip, wheat, wine

Air – Almond, baking powder, banana, bean, celery, cheese, cherry, dates, eggs, endive, figs, game, grapes, hazelnut, kumquat, mango, marjoram, mint, olives, onions, parsley, peach, pear, pecan, pine nut, pistachio, plum, poppy seeds, rice, sage, star anise, turkey, turmeric, vanilla, yogurt

Fire – Artichoke, asparagus, basil, bay, beef, beer, blackberry, black pepper, carrot, cashew, celery, chestnut, chicken, chillies, chives, chocolate, cinnamon, clove, coffee, coriander, corn, cranberry, cumin, curry, curry leaves, eggs, endive, fennel, figs, game, garlic, ginger, grapefruit, horseradish, lamb, leeks, lemongrass, lime, liver, lobster, mango, mustard, nutmeg, olives, orange, paprika, pineapple, pomegranate, pork, radish, rosemary, saffron, sesame, sunflower seed, tea, turkey, turmeric, vinegar, walnut, watercress, wine

Water – Apple, apricot, blackberry, blueberry, broccoli, Brussels sprouts, cabbage, cardamom, cauliflower, caviar, celery, cherry, coconut, coffee, crab, cranberry, cucumber, eggs, fish, game, grapefruit, grapes, gravy, honey, ice cream, kiwi fruit, lemon, lettuce, liquorice, lobster, maple syrup, margarine, melon, milk, nectarine, oil, oyster, papaya, passion fruit, peach, pear, peas, plum, poppy seeds, raspberry, soup, strawberry, sugar, sweet potato, thyme, tomato, vanilla, water, watercress, yogurt

Gender Correspondence Chart

Masculine – Almond, asparagus, banana, basil, bay, bean, beef, beer, black pepper, brazil nut, carrot, celery, cheese, chestnut, chillies, chives, cinnamon, clove, coriander, crab, cumin, curry, curry leaves, endive, fennel, game, garlic, ginger, horseradish, kiwi fruit, kumquat, lamb, leeks, lemongrass, lime, lobster, macadamia, marjoram, mint, mustard, nutmeg, olives, onions, orange, paprika, parsley, parsnip, pasta, peanut, pecan, pineapple, pine nut, pistachio, pomegranate, pork, radish, rice, rosemary, saffron, sage, sausage, sesame, star anise, sunflower seeds, tea, turkey, turnip, vinegar, walnut

Feminine – Apple, apricot, avocado, aubergine, barley, beetroot, blackberry, blueberry, bread, broccoli, Brussels sprouts, butter, cabbage, cake, cardamom, cashew, cauliflower, caviar, cherry, chicken, chocolate, coconut, coffee, corn, cranberry, cucumber, dates, fish, grapefruit, grapes, gravy, honey, ice cream, lemon, liquorice, mango, melon, milk, mushroom, nectarine, oats, papaya, passion fruit, peach, pear, peas, plum, poppy seeds, potato, pumpkin, quince, raspberry, rhubarb, rye, salt, soya, spinach, strawberry, sugar, sweet potato, thyme, tomato, turmeric, vanilla, water, watercress, wheat, yogurt

Masculine and Feminine – Artichoke, eggs, figs, hazelnut, maple syrup, oyster, wine
Neutral – Lettuce

And to a Happy Cake Filled Ending…

Food is one of my favourite subjects I love the whole process from growing it to eating it and all the processes in between. Hopefully you will have gotten a taste (yes the pun was totally intended) of how magical food can be and how easy it is to work that magic into your everyday meals and also for special occasions too.

Conversions
Although I live in the UK and most cook books and recipes give the weights in grams I love using the American 'cups' measurements, it is so easy. If you get stuck on the weights, here is a conversion chart:

Liquids

Fluid Ounces	USA	Imperial	Millilitres
1	2 tablespoons	2 tablespoons	28
2	¼ cup	4 tablespoons	56
4	½ cup	8 tablespoons	110
5		¼ pint	140
8	1 cup		225
10	1 ¼ cups	½ pint	280

Solid

Ounces	Pounds	Grams
1		28
2		56
3	½	100
4	¼	112
5		140
8	½	225
12	¾	340
16	1	450

Oven temperatures

Fahrenheit	Celsius	Gas Mark
275	140	1
300	150	2
325	170	3
350	180	4
375	190	5
400	200	6
425	220	7
450	230	8
475	240	9

Dry Goods

½ cup = 4 ounces
1 cup = 8 ounces
2 cups = 16 ounces

Ingredients

Some of the ingredients we use daily have different names in different countries, here are the basics:

Plain flour = all purpose flour
Corn flour = cornstarch
Aubergine = eggplant
Courgette = zucchini
Strong white flour = unbleached flour
Spring onion = scallion
Single cream = light cream
Double cream = heavy cream
Full fat milk = half and half

Who am I?

My Craft name is Tansy Firedragon and I have been a witch for many years now. I have studied many areas of the Craft utilising books, online resources, schools and from studying with some wonderful mentors such as Janet Farrar and Gavin Bone. I have worked through the first, second and third Wiccan Degrees.

I am High Priestess of the Kitchen Witch Coven and an Elder at the online Kitchen Witch School of Natural Witchcraft.

My Craft is a combination of old religion witchcraft, Wicca, Kitchen Witchery, green witchery and folk magic. My heart is that of a Kitchen Witch. I am blessed with a wonderful husband, lovely children, a fabulous family and good friends.

Bibliography

Pagan Portals: Kitchen Witchcraft
Grimoire of a Kitchen Witch
Pagan Portals: Hoodoo Folk Magic
Pagan Portals: Moon Magic
A Kitchen Witch's World of Magical Plants & Herbs
A Kitchen Witch's World of Magical Foods

Websites and social media
My website: www.rachelpatterson.co.uk
Facebook: www.facebook.com/rachelpattersonbooks
My personal blog: www.tansyfiredragon.blogspot.co.uk
Email: tansyfiredragon@yahoo.com
www.kitchenwitchhearth.net
www.kitchenwitchuk.blogspot.co.uk
www.facebook.com/kitchenwitchuk
www.thekitchenwitchcauldron.blogspot.co.uk

Moon Books invites you to begin or deepen your encounter with Paganism, in all its rich, creative, flourishing forms.